**Dr Cindy Pan** is a medi................................hor and media personality. S................................tice as well as sexual health an................................arly appears on television as well as lecturing, speaking and writing about health, lifestyle and relationship issues. Cindy is the author of *Pandora's Box: lifting the lid on life's little nasties*, a book about health, relationships, sex and drugs; as well as *Playing Hard to Get* about dating in the twenty-first century. She lives in Sydney and has two young children.

**Vanessa Woods** is an internationally published Australian author and journalist, and is currently a Research Scientist at Duke University in North Carolina. A graduate of the Australian National University with a Masters degree in Science Communication, and an author of children's books, Vanessa is best known for her research and work comparing the different cooperative behaviours of bonobos and chimpanzees. She is the author of *It's Every Monkey for Themselves* and *Bonobo Handshake*.

*For my darlings, Anton and Jeremy,*
*with all my love, Cindy-Mummy*

# Headstarts

100 tips for raising clever,
confident, creative kids

**Dr Cindy Pan and Vanessa Woods**

ALLEN&UNWIN

First published in Australia in 2011

Allen & Unwin
Sydney, Melbourne,
Auckland, London

83 Alexander Street
Crows Nest NSW 2065
Australia
Phone:     (61 2) 8425 0100
Fax:       (61 2) 9906 2218
Email:     info@allenandunwin.com
Web:       www.allenandunwin.com

Cataloguing-in-Publication details are available
from the National Library of Australia
www.trove.nla.gov.au

ISBN 978 174175 574 9

Typeset in 12/14.5 Adobe Garamond by Midland Typesetters, Maryborough
Printed and bound in Australia by McPherson's Printing Group

10 9 8 7 6 5 4 3 2 1

MIX
Paper from
responsible sources
FSC
www.fsc.org
FSC® C001695

The paper in this book is FSC certified.
FSC promotes environmentally responsible,
socially beneficial and economically viable
management of the world's forests.

# Contents

# Introduction

Each year there are thousands of studies published about children. It's one of the best-funded, most influential fields of psychology because most people believe, like Whitney Houston once sang, that children are our future.

However, those studies are published in journals that can cost thousands of dollars a year to subscribe to. Occasionally a really big study will make it into the mainstream media, but then you're relying on journalistic spin to decipher it. And then there are all those other studies that get buried in obscure journals that libraries keep in their basements.

We know that today's parents have a million things to do between breakfast and bedtime. We know you want the facts, and so we're bringing them to you, free of both scientific jargon and tabloid fear-mongering.

Most of the studies drawn on in this book have been published in recent years. Things change, ideas evolve, and some of what might have been commonly accepted in your parents' day (like the idea that sugar makes kids hyper or that Mozart makes them smarter) has been debunked in the new millennium. Some of these studies may well be debunked in the next few decades too, but we've aimed to give you what's current, credible and likely to last the distance. In the interest of readability, we've dropped a lot of the cans, mights, probablys and possiblys that scientists love using. Hardly anything in science is concrete, and most of it is debatable, including many of the things we report here. But even so, these studies have all been published in well-respected, peer-reviewed journals, so you're getting the best of what's out there.

We know that school is becoming more competitive, and you no doubt want your kids to do well. So many of our tips are geared towards giving your kids that little edge in school to get them ahead. But we also know you want your kids to make it to their eighteenth birthday, and to be happy and healthy when they do, so we've also included the latest findings on safety, emotional intelligence and nutrition.

Most of all, we want you to know that you're a great parent and you're doing a fabulous job. These little headstarts are supposed to be like washing machines and vacuum cleaners were to previous generations of parents—making your life easier so you can concentrate on having more fun with your kids.

Love,

*Cindy and Vanessa*

# 1. Don't be too hard on yourself

'It's got to be-ee-ee-ee, perfect . . .' goes the popular eighties' song where a woman sets out the conditions for all her future relationships. Good luck, honey!

For career mums juggling the dual roles of worker and mother, being a perfectionist can be a recipe for stress, depression, conflict and lower overall satisfaction with themselves and life.

Of course there are lots of rewards (such as the thrill of achieving) that come from perfectionist behaviour, features of which might include being organised, hard-working and committed to your goals. But sometimes perfectionists are motivated by guilt, fear of failure, or fear of others' disappointment or censure rather than the rewards of a job well done. It is when the fear of negative consequences is greater than the lure of positive ones that this form of perfectionism becomes less healthy, leading to decreased satisfaction and leaving the perfectionist vulnerable to dejection, shame, embarrassment and a generally low mood.

It is important for mums, especially career mums, not to put too much pressure on themselves to be perfect and to realise that sometimes the best outcomes will be achieved by aiming for 'good enough'. Most importantly, setting realistic standards and having the satisfaction of defining and achieving *your own* goals rather than any socially prescribed standards is the key to a less stressful existence.

[Jacqueline K. Mitchelson, Lawrence R. Burns, 'Career mothers and perfectionism: stress at work and at home', *Personality and Individual Differences, 25*, 1998, pp. 477–485.]

## 2. Is one too many?

Everyone has their own opinion about if and how much women should drink during pregnancy, and the research is no different. If you want a research paper that says drinking a few glasses of wine per week is fine, you can find it. If you want one saying that even one glass a week can cause serious behavioural and academic problems, you can find that too.

What we know for sure is that heavy drinking causes Foetal Alcohol Syndrome, which is the leading cause of mental retardation in the Western world. Some symptoms of FAS are stunted growth, facial deformity and brain damage. What researchers can't decide on is whether 'heavy drinking' is one glass of wine a week or four.

Foetal Alcohol Syndrome isn't all you have to worry about when a glass of wine feels tempting. One study we looked at showed that even drinking one glass of wine a week increased the chances of having a child with depression and a lower IQ (particularly in mathematics).

However, another study showed that mothers who drank between one and two glasses of wine a week had boys with less behaviour problems and girls with less emotional and peer problems.

The problem is that nothing works in isolation. Maybe mothers who drink a couple of glasses of wine a week are more likely to be less rigid in other areas, like discipline and encouraging academic achievement. Maybe these same mothers are less stressed and more willing to take care of themselves and their needs, which has a positive impact on their kids.

So the facts as far as we know are: drinking four glasses of wine a week while pregnant can definitely cause serious damage, and a couple of glasses a week could be either harmful or not. The choice of what to believe, and what to do, is up to you.

[K.K. Howell et al., 'Prenatal alcohol exposure and ability, academic achievement, and school functioning in adolescence: a longitudinal follow-up', *Journal of Pediatric Psychology*, 31 (1), 2006, pp. 116–26. Y. Kelly et al., 'Light drinking in pregnancy, a risk for behavioural problems and cognitive deficits at 3 years of age?', *International Journal of Epidemiology*, 38 (1), 2009, pp. 129–40. M.J.P. O'Connor, 'The relationship of prenatal alcohol exposure and the postnatal environment to child depressive symptoms', *Journal of Pediatric Psychology*, 31, pp. 50–64.]

## 3. Get clean

We're assuming no one who buys this book is likely to be snorting coke off their coffee table, but just in case you are one of the 3.4 million Australians who are daily smokers or one of the three million Australians who have taken illicit drugs in the last twelve months, this hint is for you.

If you are pregnant, thinking about getting pregnant, or think you might be pregnant, you have to clean up your act. No last E at one last dance party, no goodbye cigarette. The days of carefree experimentation are over, at least for you.

All drugs will damage your baby's development, some in ways we haven't yet discovered. For instance, ecstasy has been linked with cardiovascular and musculoskeletal deformities in babies whose mothers took the drug during pregnancy. Prenatal marijuana use is related to hyperactivity, problems with attention and delinquency in children as old as ten.

Taking cocaine even occasionally when you are pregnant can severely affect the language skills of children for the first six years of their life. Although after that the kids may catch up, language skills help kids settle into school and make friends. Delays in language development can lead to social awkwardness, as well as low test scores. Using cocaine while pregnant has also been linked to poor attention, lower IQ, and poor motor skills.

Warning signs plastered over cigarette packets tell you that smoking is bad for your baby, but they don't say how. Cigarette smoke has over 2500 chemicals, with carbon monoxide, nicotine and tar the most toxic to your baby's health. Smoking can cause miscarriage, stillbirth and severe vaginal bleeding. Your baby has a one in ten chance of being premature, which increases the risk of cerebral palsy, mental retardation, learning disabilities, asthma and, last but not least, Sudden Infant Death Syndrome (SIDS).

Get smart and get clean. It's not just about you now.

[M. Beeghly et al., 'Prenatal cocaine exposure and children', Language Functioning at 6 and 9.5 Years: Moderating Effects of Child Age, Birthweight, and Gender. *Journal of Pediatric Psychology, 31* (1), 98–115. F.D. Gilliland et al., 'Effects of maternal smoking during pregnancy and environmental tobacco smoke on asthma and wheezing in children', *Am. J. Respir. Crit. Care Med., 163* (2), 2001, pp. 429–36. S.C.J. Huijbregts et al., 'Interrelations between maternal smoking during pregnancy, birth weight and sociodemographic factors in the prediction of early cognitive abilities', *Infant and Child Development, 15* (6), 2006, pp. 593–607. J.V. Pham & T. Puzantian, *Ecstasy: Dangers and controversies,* (Vol. 21), Boston, MA, ETATS-UNIS: Pharmacotherapy. S.J. Roza et al., 'Maternal smoking during pregnancy and child behaviour problems: the Generation R study', *International Journal of Epidemiology, 38* (3), 2009, pp. 680–9. K. Wisborg et al., 'A prospective study of smoking during pregnancy and SIDS', *Archives of Disease in Childhood, 83* (3), 2000, pp. 203–6.]

## 4. Demand feeding: breast and beyond

Along with providing the best source of nutrition for around the first six months of a child's life, breastmilk reduces the risk of infectious and chronic digestive diseases in infants. Less well recognised is the role breastfeeding can play in modifying or balancing maternal control over how a child eats long after they're weaned.

Previous research has shown that highly controlling feeding strategies can have a negative impact on babies' and children's ability to adjust their intake in response to the energy content of foods. High levels of parental control over what and how much their children eat is also associated with greater fat levels in kids and a heightened desire for and increased consumption of those fabulous forbidden foods.

Infants eat primarily to satisfy energy needs. The advantage of breastfeeding is that, since the mother cannot readily determine the exact volume her baby drinks, the quantity consumed is largely determined by the infant, with the mother assuming that the baby is sated when sucking stops. With bottlefeeding the mother may be guided by how much is left in the bottle, encouraging the baby to keep feeding until the bottle is empty—the infant equivalent of 'finishing what's on your plate' regardless of the child's innate, instinctual sense of fullness.

Current research suggests that mothers who breastfeed for the first year of their child's life learn something crucial about how the child can—and should—play a role in regulating their own nutritional intake. Demand feeding practices in particular make a mother more responsive to her infant's cues and enhance shared mother–infant responsibility, not just in early babyhood but well into the toddler period.

Breastfed babies may also be exposed to a far greater variety of flavours and odours from their mum's diet via breastmilk compared to babies given only commercial formula preparations. This seems to have a positive influence on the baby's subsequent acceptance of a greater variety of solid foods, since effectively he or she may have 'tasted' them at the nipple.

Women who breastfed for a year or more needed to exert less control over their chilren's eating habits later, and while their kids had higher energy intakes, they were taller and leaner (but not heavier) as toddlers.

Even if breastfeeding was not for you, it's good to share the responsibility for healthy eating with your toddler, young child and teenager. In doing so you should generally avoid using 'treats' or desserts as rewards for eating 'good but nasty-tasting' food; enforcing rules about clearing the plate; making children eat when they're not hungry; inflexibly refusing children food when they are hungry just because it doesn't fit with an arbitrary schedule; chiding them for eating too much or too little or the wrong thing at the wrong time; reprimanding them for playing with their food instead of simply chowing down like eating machines, regardless of whether or not they feel hungry or like the food. Some or all of these examples of parental control over feeding can end up teaching kids to override their own hunger and fullness cues.

The best tool we each have for guiding energy and nutrient intake is our own innate sense of hunger and fullness. Babies and toddlers know how much is enough and, left to their own devices, they will neither starve nor gorge excessively. We need to trust our kids to develop their own sense of self-regulation to avoid burdening them with our generation's often problematic, overly restrictive and self-punitive approach to food. So relax. If they're hungry, let them eat; if they're not, let them be.

[Jennifer O. Fisher et al., 'Breast-feeding through the first year predicts maternal control in feeding and subsequent toddler energy intakes', *Journal of the American Dietetic Association*, vol. 100, no. 6, June 2000.]

# 5. Laughter, the breast medicine

It seems like a good chortle before breastfeeding can be beneficial to babies, especially if they are allergy prone and suffer from allergic eczema.

It has been found that allergic eczema is frequently associated with chronic stress, sleep disturbance and decreased levels of a hormone called melatonin (involved in sleep and stress responses). It is thought that relaxation by laughter may increase melatonin levels which may, in turn, reduce allergic responses.

According to one study, laughing before breastfeeding increases the levels of melatonin in breastmilk, and infants drinking this melatonin-boosted milk have been shown to have reduced allergic responses (as measured by skin wheal reactions to common allergies such as house mite dust and latex).

Women who watched humorous DVDs (such as a Charlie Chaplin movie) as opposed to non-humorous ones (such as weather information) produced breastmilk with significantly higher melatonin levels and their babies' skin reactions to common allergens were significantly decreased. It seems that watching Dawn French, Benny Hill, Basil Fawlty and the Chaser Boys, not only gives you a good laugh, but can also beautify your baby's complexion.

[Hajime Kimata, 'Laughter elevates the levels of breast-milk melatonin', *Journal of Psychosomatic Research*, 62, 2007, pp. 699–702.]

## 6. Breast is best

Your nipples are chafed and raw. Your boobs ache. The teeth pushing through those little gums are leaving scars. Not only that, you fantasise about leaving the baby with your mother for a month so you can get a good night's sleep.

Breastfeeding, although supposed to epitomise the unique connection between mother and child, can sometimes be a pain in the, well, breast. But if you are finding it uncomfortable, fight the temptation to switch to the bottle before your baby is six months old because breastmilk is important to your baby's development and health, especially if they have a version of a gene called FADS2.

The FADS2 gene is involved with processing fatty acids, which in turn helps brain development and function, although no one knows the exact mechanism by which this happens. Children with this particular genetic variant (and most do have it) who are breastfed can gain seven points of IQ.

> Breastfed children attain higher IQ scores than children not fed breast milk, presumably because of the fatty acids uniquely available in breast milk. The association between breastfeeding and IQ is moderated by a genetic variant in FADS2, a gene involved in the genetic control of fatty acid pathways. Children with the 'C' version of the gene (90 per cent of the 3000 children in the study) had an IQ advantage of about 6 to 7 points, regardless of the mother's socioeconomic status and birth weight of the baby.

[A. Caspi et al., 'Moderation of breastfeeding effects on the IQ by genetic variation in fatty acid metabolism', *104* (47), 2007, p. 6.]

## 7. Childproof everything!

All parents occasionally wonder whether their children are deliberately trying to ruin years of careful decorating with suicidal tendencies. From falling off fashionably high bar stools to cracking their heads on the art deco coffee table, children seem determined to run right into the least child-safe area of the room and hurt themselves so you have to ruin the decor with childproofing.

Unfortunately, we aren't born knowing that sharp edges hurt when you fall on them, that swimming pools are death traps, or that cutlery and power outlets don't mix. We have to learn this information, and it takes a while to absorb it all.

Take heights. When babies who have just started to crawl are put on top of a 1.3-metre-high 'cliff', they crawl right off it (luckily, in the experiment a transparent piece of plexiglass stops them from actually falling). Newly mobile, babies haven't learnt what a steep drop looks like, or what it means.

That's why you have to put railings on the balcony, lock the gate to the pool, and cover the sharp corners of your lovely coffee table with ugly foam padding. At what age can you return your house to the Vogue Living version originally intended? It's different for every child. But no one knows them better than you, and you're the one most likely to notice when the penny finally drops about hairdryers not making good bath toys.

For at least the first few years, your children need you to look out for them until they develop the wisdom to look out for themselves.

[D.C. Witherington et al., 'Avoidance of heights on the visual cliff in newly walking infants', *Infancy*, 7 (3), 2005, pp. 285–98.]

## 8. The modern dilemma for new mums

Some women who return to work and place their children in care feel guilty about their choice and may believe others disapprove of their decision. Women who return to work 'early', say within three to six months of childbirth, may experience even greater guilt and feel others judge them or their decision harshly.

In one study, women were interviewed to explore their views, feelings and reasons for returning to work and placing their babies in a variety of types of care from a childcare centre to a nanny, friend, grandparent or other relative.

A woman's decision to return to work after having a child can be influenced by a wide range of factors, including financial need, career development goals and fear of job loss. In general, women from lower socioeconomic backgrounds understandably tend to cite extra income as the main reason for returning to work, whereas women with higher incomes, more education and higher occupational status were more likely to emphasise career goals and enjoyment of work.

In this particular study, children were in non-maternal care for anything from 12 to 53 hours per week (the highest number of hours was with a grandparent as carer), the average being around 30 hours per week. The factors which most influenced mothers' final selection of type of child care were location, convenience, cost and availability. Other important factors included flexibility, the personality and experience of the potential carer, adult/child ratios and group numbers, provision of learning and/or social experiences, safety aspects, recommendations and advice from others, the infant's age and emotional well-being, and how supportive the father or partner was.

Some men encouraged their wives to go back to work, believing that it would be good for both their partner and their baby to have contact with other people. Other men considered giving up work and looking after the baby themselves, particularly if their wife earned more. Either way, as a couple they felt they could not afford for the mother not to return to work.

For many women, retaining 'sanity' and keeping their career going were more influential than financial gain in their decision to return to work—often after child care, travel and other costs were added they were only breaking even. For others it was not so much enjoyment of work as wanting the independence of having their own money again. Some women had pledged to return to work within a certain time period and felt obliged to honour that commitment. Not wanting to have to start all over again from the bottom, feeling uncomfortable about not working, and wanting to do something 'constructive' and have contact with 'grown-ups' were other factors driving women back to work.

As far as the type of child care chosen went, a diversity of rationales was revealed. While some actively sought a carer who would develop a strong, one-on-one relationship with their child, others specifically wanted a group setting so that they would not have to 'share' the one-on-one relationship they had with their baby with a single carer. Others felt that there would be more stimulation in a childcare setting since individual carers might spend unknown numbers of hours watching television or doing their own housework.

The mothers' remarks about their partners' involvement in decision-making were also interesting. While almost half the women said they discussed childcare arrangements with the baby's father, only 3 per cent said their partner had any actual direct influence on their choice. Mostly the father's role was one of confirming the mother's choice rather than having his own strong view. In general, men tended to be either compliant or disengaged. In 6 per cent of cases the mothers described their decisions as having been made irrespective of the partner's views.

While around 54 per cent of women felt happy that the childcare choice they had made at the beginning still felt right, 31 per cent volunteered uncomfortable feelings about some aspect of their current childcare situation or working lifestyle with key themes being guilt (particularly in regard to ceasing breastfeeding), concern about the baby's well-being, anxiety about loss of control of their baby's life and upbringing, and ambivalence about their work–mothering balance.

The study found that mothers would benefit from more reliable information and education regarding the characteristics and importance of high-quality child care, whatever the setting, as well as information regarding attachment to give them more confidence about their own central place in their child's world and to relieve any unnecessary distress about being supplanted from their prime position by another caregiver.

Mothers tended to readily accept care from relatives

or friends because they were 'known', without considering the importance of a home receiving regular safety checks or any individual being police-checked (which are standard procedures in any formal child care environment). Many did not seek or follow up references for nannies or au pairs either.

Interestingly, women were highly influenced—invariably negatively so—by media coverage of abuse or neglect by nannies or childcare workers, despite their rarity when compared with the much more commonplace examples of good childcare practice.

Finally, too many women left it to the last minute to arrange child care such that they ended up being less than satisfied with their choices.

There's a lot to consider in all this, so if you're planning to return to work after childbirth it's worth thinking about the different options during pregnancy to create more choices for yourself. Visiting childcare centres, interviewing, assessing and researching other carer options and getting on waiting lists early is worthwhile, as is seeking advice from health professionals regarding features to consider in various childcare settings. Most importantly, women need to feel reassured that regardless of their choices, they remain in control as prime carers who can and should work cooperatively and collaboratively with whoever they choose to care for their child.

[Penelope Leach et al., 'Child care before 6 months of age: A qualitative study of mothers' decisions and feelings about employment and non-maternal care', *Infant and Child Development*, vol. 15, 2006, pp. 471–502.]

## 9. Hi ho, hi ho, it's back to work you go

That young high-flyer at the office is going to take over your job if you don't get back soon. You'll go crazy with no one to talk to but a baby. You've just spent the last nine months being sick, fat, and in pain, and you can't wait to get back to normal life.

As compelling as these reasons might seem to you now, if there is any way you can swing it, stay home and bond with your baby for the first nine months after they are born.

The reality is that most women work and, for a variety of reasons, will continue working while they have children. While some workplaces are extremely progressive, others are snarky and completely insensitive to the pressures and responsibilities of being a mother.

But the best child care in the world can't compensate for what your child really needs—you. No one can scientifically quantify the magical bond between a mother and child, but the upshot is that children whose mothers return to work before they are nine months old suffer in terms of Bracken School Readiness (51 tests that assess a child's knowledge of colour, letter identification, mathematics, comparisons and shape recognition). This can affect them during the first three years of life.

If for financial or other reasons you can't manage the time off, talk to your boss about going part time. Money is important for your children, but not as important as you.

[J. Brooks–Gunn et al., 'Maternal employment and child cognitive outcomes in the first three years of life: the NICHD study of early child care', *Child Development, 73* (4), 2002, pp. 1052–72.]

## 10. Chill out

We get it. You have 286 things to do between breakfast and brushing your teeth. You barely have time to pee, much less spend an hour doing yoga, shoe shopping, or all the other self-absorbed activities you could do before you had kids.

But factoring in some kind of down time that will decrease your stress level is important. Of course, life is always throwing curve balls that are guaranteed to stress you, but this is about the kind of stress you might regain control over if you give yourself some time out. For instance, feeling alone, doubting your child-raising abilities, having frequent fights with your partner, or feeling unappreciated.

This kind of 'parenting stress' can lead to your kids having poor social skills and behaviour problems in pre-school. Teachers report that children who live with stressed parents have problems adjusting to the classroom, socialising, and tend to be withdrawn and anxious.

So whether it's regular exercise, a massage, or catch-up time with girlfriends or family, make it a priority. Or try to factor a babysitter into your budget so you can have some 'me' time. Getting away from your kids for a while so you can regroup might be the best thing for them.

[L.G. Anthony et al., 'The relationships between parenting stress, parenting behaviour and preschoolers' social competence and behaviour problems in the classroom', *Infant and Child Development, 14* (2), 2005, pp. 133–54.]

## 11. Spend quality time

Many women have a tendency to multi-task, talking on the phone while doing the dishes while listening to the evening news. Making lunch while eating breakfast while letting the dog out to pee.

Often it's tempting to multi-task with your baby, especially since they don't move much and you can just pop them somewhere nearby while you write your emails, read the paper, do the laundry, and so on. But make sure you squeeze in quality time, and not just ten minutes before dinner. We're talking time each day, several times a day where you aren't doing anything but paying attention to your baby. Tickle their toes, tell them stories, or just make funny faces. And keep spending time with them as they grow older.

We don't know why, but this quality time helps your baby's brain develop. 'Secure' mothers who are warm, responsive and engaged have children with higher IQs, better verbal skills and less behavioural problems than 'insecure' (disinterested, defensive or dismissive) mothers.

*Children of warm responsive mothers scored 19 points higher on a standardized version of the Stanford-Binet Intelligence Scale than did children of disinterested or dismissive mothers. This difference was significant even after the influence of maternal IQ, education, and family socio economic status were taken into account.*

[L.E. Crandell & R.P. Hobson, 'Individual differences in young children's IQ: a social-developmental perspective', *Journal of Child Psychology and Psychiatry*, *40* (3), 1999, pp. 455–64.]

## 12. Take care of your emotional, spiritual and mental health

As a mother, it's natural to want to put your child first. Sometimes we get so caught up in doing the best for our children, we do it at the cost of what we need to stay happy. Not only that, but we tend to put ourselves last, believing that it doesn't matter if we feel sad or depressed, as long as everyone else is taken care of.

But the best thing you can do for your child is to make sure you have the things you need to stay mentally healthy. Whether that means leaning on your family and friends for support, having a night out with the girls every now and then, or going to see a professional who can help you untangle your thoughts and emotions.

You often hear that kids are sponges, soaking up information and absorbing it. It's important to know that they are also sponges emotionally. If you are depressed, your children will suffer. Children of depressed mothers have more behavioural problems, slower cognitive development, and are more withdrawn and irritable than children of non-depressed mothers. They also have more negative emotions and vocalise less.

Your depression may even alter their brain activity. Children of depressed mothers have less activity in the left frontal region of the brain, responsible for joy and interest, and more activity in the right frontal regions which are responsible for withdrawal emotions like sadness.

You are the most important person in your child's life. Try to relax and have fun. Eliminate the stresses that decrease your quality of life. If you suffer from chronic depression, your doctor can help. Take care of yourself. Your kids will end up better for it.

[G. Dawson et al., 'Preschool outcomes of children of depressed mothers: role of maternal behaviour, contextual risk, and children's brain activity', *Child Development, 74* (4), 2003, pp. 1158–75.]

## 13. Enjoy their joy

It has been said that when you share your woes you decrease them and when you share your joys you increase them. However, it really depends on who you share them with.

Research shows that young adolescents whose mothers don't respond enthusiastically to their displays of positive emotions—such as joy, pride, excitement or curiosity—report more depressive symptoms. They may also have greater difficulty regulating their emotions generally and can be drawn into a sad or depressed state they find difficult to get out of.

Adolescence is a time of particular risk for the onset of depressive disorders, so understanding how emotional regulation skills develop is important in prevention and early intervention for kids with these tendencies.

Family environment plays a crucial role, and some studies suggest that poor familial relationships have an even stronger association with depressive symptoms in adolescents than peer relationships. Conversely, parents who frequently and readily discuss both positive and negative emotions (including explaining the causes and consequences of emotions and reactions to their kids' expressed emotions) tend to have kids with better emotional skills in early childhood, which is in turn associated with better emotional regulation skills in adolescence.

If a mother regularly responds to her child's high spirits by saying 'Be quiet!' or 'Sit down and shut up!', the child may learn to suppress feelings of happiness and joy and fail to learn better ways to regulate their positive emotions and moods.

This can potentially lead to emotional flatness and an inability to react or feel things properly, where even good news brings no brightening of mood. Boys are more likely to reciprocate their mum's aversive (contemptuous, angry belligerent, disapproving, threatening or argumentative) reactions, whereas girls tend to reciprocate their mum's dysphoric (anxious, whining, complaining or self-derogatory) behaviour.

Such mothers' behaviour doesn't necessarily relate to a clinically depressive state on their part, but rather indicates that there is something out of kilter in the relationship between the mother and her child. And though mum's the adult, it does take two to tango.

Parents need to be aware that preventing or stifling a kid's expression of positive feelings can have a real impact on their emotional development and state of mind. Parents who are accepting and supportive, and who offer or provide coaching and problem solving approaches to assist when their kids are feeling down, tend to have children with fewer depressive symptoms and more adaptive responses to feeling down.

So be happy that they're happy, even if you're not feeling so flash yourself. Slap on a smiling face and have a laugh with them. It might cheer you up and, even if it doesn't, the alternative is even sadder.

[Marie B.H. Yap et al., 'Maternal socialization of positive affect: The impact of invalidation on adolescent emotion regulation and depressive symptomatology', *Child Development*, vol. 79, no. 5, Sept/Oct 2008, pp. 1415–31.]

## 14. Happy parents, happy kids?

Conflict and disharmony between parents can be difficult to deal with. No one chooses to have a bad relationship or to expose their kids to the destructive, violent or abusive consequences of one. But discord between parents is a real public health concern.

Being exposed to high levels of conflict at home can leave kids vulnerable to a broad range of psychological issues, from depression and anxiety to aggression, poor peer relations and academic difficulties. Witnessing discord between parents can heighten kids' concerns about preserving their security, and while this may be a sensible or even necessary response, this sharpened sensitivity to potential threats comes at a cost: including the possibility of long-term maladaptive psychological functioning.

A recent study looked at school adjustment, performance and problems in six year olds. It used ratings of kids' insecure representations of their parents' relationships to predict the presence, degree or absence of attention difficulties and other school problems over a one-year period.

Just how attention difficulties are linked to school adjustment problems is complex, but research suggests that kids with attention difficulties are at increased risk of problems with behaviour, friendships and academic achievement. The study showed that kids who are insecure about their parents' relationship have greater attention difficulties, which were in turn associated with ongoing and increasing problems at school.

Why? Perhaps because kids who think their home life is in trouble are primed to look for and interpret other challenging settings as similar threats. Or perhaps it's because so many of their mental and emotional resources are being taken up with concerns for their security that their ability to persevere on other challenging tasks is compromised, along with their ability to engage in academic and social undertakings, behave appropriately and comply with rules, especially in the face of distraction or boredom.

There are three clear lessons from this:

1. Parents in high-conflict relationships need to be aware of the potential and specific damage and dangers their behaviour may be inflicting on their children and, where possible, take preventive measures, be it couples or individual therapy, family therapy or, failing that, more definitive measures such as separation.
2. Kids' concerns about security need to be understood and acknowledged, but not always with a view to altering them. These concerns may in fact be providing them with an effective way to identify and cope with conflict before any threat of danger escalates.
3. Programs and measures designed to assist kids to optimise their attention processes in social and academic settings are important, as they may help protect kids from potential negative outcomes.

You can't necessarily eliminate parental discord, although ideally you should try to minimise it, and you can't necessarily stop affected kids from having heightened security concerns (indeed to do so may even be harmful) but to whatever degree we can intervene to enhance kids' attention skills we may be able to moderate otherwise potentially very damaging effects.

[Patrick T. Davies et al., 'Children's insecure representations of the inter-parental relationship and their school adjustment: the mediating role of attention difficulties', *Child Development*, vol. 79, no. 5, Sept/Oct 2008, pp. 1570–82.]

## 15. First love

For most of us, the first loving relationship in our lives was with our mum.

The three general styles of mother–infant attachment are: secure (when mum is sensitive and responsive to her infant's signals and responses), avoidant (when the mother constantly rebuffs the infant's efforts to establish physical contact) and anxious/ambivalent (when mums are slow or inconsistent in their responses to their infant's cries or force attention on to the child without being tuned in to their needs). Some psychologists theorise that the different models of self and social life established in this early relationship stay with us from cradle to grave.

According to a wealth of research, the two key factors that determine a person's expectations about having their needs met, are laid down in our first few years of life. They are:

1. whether we believe the person we're attached to will, in general, respond to our calls for support and protection, and;
2. whether we believe that we, ourselves, are loving and lovable.

Is it possible that the way we bond with our babies in those first months and years affects the nature and course of their emotional attachments and romantic relationships for life?

A recent study quizzed adult men and women on a range of topics, from their assumptions, expectations and beliefs about romantic love to their memories of childhood experiences with mum. Results revealed that the proportions of adults whose early relationship with their mother was characterised as secure (56 per cent), anxious/ambivalent (19 per cent) or avoidant (25 per cent) were very similar to the proportions reported in previous studies of infants (62 per cent, 15 per cent and 23 per cent respectively).

The secure adults described their most important love experiences as especially happy, friendly and trusting, placing an emphasis on being able to accept and support their partner despite any faults. By contrast, those who had avoidant relationships with their mother described adult relationships characterised by fear of intimacy, emotional highs and lows, jealousy, and overall less positive love experiences. Those who had anxious/ambivalent relationships with their mother experienced adult love as involving obsession, desire for reciprocation and union, emotional highs and lows, and extreme sexual attraction and jealousy. They also scored highest on loneliness, yearning for a love relationship but having difficulty finding willing partners.

As adults, those whose early attachment with their mother was secure tended to have relationships that lasted longer, and only a 6 per cent divorce rate compared with 12 per cent for avoidant-background adults and 10 per cent for those with anxious/ambivalent early relationships. Interestingly, there was no correlation between attachment type and either parental divorce or duration of any separations from parents during childhood. The main factor predicting each individual's attachment type was simply the quality of their relationship with their mother and the parents' relationship with each other.

While it would be naïve to suggest that relationships and behavioural styles adopted in infancy remain completely unchanged throughout life, clearly everything has its beginnings somewhere and certain early influences do seem to have enduring effects.

While study results do support the concept of continuity of attachment style from infancy to adulthood, the correlations tend to be stronger for younger adults, suggesting that continuity decreases as one gets further into adulthood with influential intervening experiences such as friendships and relationships playing an increasingly significant role.

In terms of whether one's own attachment affects the style of attachment one is likely to engender in one's own offspring, research suggests that while there is some association, many parents do manage to break the pattern, with adults, for example, who themselves felt insecure in their relationships with their parents managing to produce securely attached infants and children. The way we bond with our kids from infancy, our continued sensitivity towards our ongoing relationships and the nature of our children's subsequent relationships will all have an impact on their future loving and romantic relationships. Our job is to love them as well as we can for as long as we can and hope that this sets them on the right path.

[Cindy Hazan & Phillip Shaver, 'Romantic love conceptualised as an attachment process', *Journal of Personality and Social Psychology*, vol. 52, no. 3, 1987, pp. 511–24.]

## 16. Hugs help their brains to grow

The touch of another human being is something we all crave, but this is especially true for children. Infants bond to their mothers from birth, and physical contact mysteriously leads to emotional development that happens in the brain.

Arginine vasopressin (AVP) is the hormone that helps us form social bonds and increase our positive social interactions (as well as form memories of these interactions.) Children who are raised without much human contact in places like orphanages have lower AVP than other children.

Children who experience early neglect also have low levels of oxytocin, a hormone that makes infants feel secure and protected. Neglected children are difficult to calm and often have social problems. Even when the children are moved to loving homes, the early years of neglect mean the damage has been done.

So hug your children often. They can't get enough.

[A.B. Wismer Fries et al., 'Early experience in humans is associated with changes in neuropeptides critical for regulating social behavior', *PNAS*, 102 (47), 2005, p. 4.]

## 17. They can't walk or talk but they can watch and listen

They are so new they can't even lift their heads up. They don't do much of anything besides drink, poop and vomit. But this doesn't mean your baby doesn't know who you are, or that they aren't paying attention to you.

In fact, they know exactly who you are. The ability of babies to recognise their mothers is something so special that science has a hard time explaining it. Even a few hours after birth, babies recognise and prefer the face of their mother to anyone else.

By the time they are three months old, they are constantly paying attention to you—to your voice, to your face, to the silly little games you play that you sometimes feel you're playing on your own.

So enjoy all the attention. Right now, you're the most important person in the world.

[A. Slater & P.C. Quinn, 'Face recognition in the newborn infant,' *Infant and Child Development*, 10 (1–2), 2001, pp. 21–4. T. Striano, A. Henning, & D. Stahl, 'Sensitivity to social contingencies between 1 and 3 months of age,' *Developmental Science*, 8 (6), 2005, pp. 509–18.]

## 18. Motherese

There's a reason why most of us instinctively raise our voices five pitches and talk nonsense whenever a baby is put in front of us. Babies need time for their hearing to develop. They generally start learning language when they are between twelve and eighteen months old. Before that, they rely on tone, pitch, sound patterns and inflections.

The exaggerated pitches and slow sounds mothers make are a special language that lets the baby know they should be soothed, paying attention, or not doing whatever they are doing.

'Motherese' is a precursor to language. So when you say 'gooooood baby' or 'nooooo' in that exaggerated sing song voice your baby is slowly getting the hang of words like 'good' and 'no'.

So don't let anyone tell you to talk to your baby like they are an adult. Babies pay more attention when you speak motherese than if you try to talk to them normally. 'Cootchie cootchie coo' is as important as ABC.

[E.V. Clark, 'How language acquisition builds on cognitive development,' *Trends in Cognitive Sciences, 8* (10), 2004, pp. 472–8. R.I. Sokol, et al., 'Whining as mother-directed speech,' *Infant and Child Development, 14* (5), 2005, pp. 478–90.]

## 19. It's not all talk when it comes to babies

The use of gestures by babies is now recognised as the true beginnings of language. Which means all that flapping and pointing that's going on is really your pre-verbal baby trying to communicate with you.

Though sign language is generally seen as a tool for the deaf, encouraging hearing children to use sign language, in addition to babbling and talking, enhances communication and helps with speech development.

In one study, a group of parents was encouraged to promote signing by modelling simple gestures while saying the associated words. The infants in this group were then compared with infants who were given either 'no intervention' or whose parents simply made special efforts to repeatedly emphasise the name of objects or actions. The infants who had been encouraged to sign learnt to use a multitude of symbolic gestures spontaneously, plus they were able to express surprisingly detailed observations, revealing abilities that would otherwise have gone undetected.

Signing benefits language development in several ways:

1. It increases an infant's repertoire of communication, making them more able to respond to what grown-ups are saying.
2. It allows little ones to start communicating and eliciting responses sooner, which means grown-ups will probably talk to them more, which speeds up language acquisition.

3. As your infant is better able to direct things when they're doing the signing, conversation is more likely to focus on what they're interested in. And just like adults, infants pay more attention to things that they are interested in.

4. Increasing the number of things they can spontaneously indicate increases the odds you'll be able to figure out what they want. And as any parent of a whining, pre-verbal infant or toddler can attest, it's frustrating trying to figure out what it is they want when they can't tell you! By encouraging signing, it is more likely your little one will be able to let you know their needs and have these needs met without having to dissolve in a flood of tears or fling themselves on the supermarket floor.

5. It allows infants to learn concepts, for example, moving his hand in a certain way can make you get him a drink!

The good news is that children's language will develop regardless of any signing. A lot of gesturing is intuitive anyway, like waving good bye, or nodding for yes and shaking for no.

If you're interested in trying signing, it's really quite easy and, more importantly, fun. You can learn an established sign language such as Auslan or simply adapt and adopt any kinds of signs or gestures that make sense for you. So long as you're reasonably consistent with the gestures you use and you can remember them, it will work just fine.

Of course, symbolic gestures are not meant to *replace* speech. On the contrary, signing appears to jump-start verbal development. That's got to get a big thumbs up. So no pressure now: just relax and enjoy 'talking' to your baby.

[Susan Goodwyn et al., 'Impact of symbolic gesturing on early language development' *Journal of Nonverbal Behaviour* 24 (2), Summer 2000, pp. 81–103.]

## 20. To cry or not to cry?

There's so much conflicting information about how to put your baby to bed it's almost as if you're diffusing a nuclear bomb. Will cuddling your baby to sleep make them hopelessly dependent? If you let them cry themselves to sleep will they develop an anxiety disorder?

Various studies show that babies whose parents smother them with hugs and kisses before putting them to bed tend to have more sleeping problems than those whose parents just give them a quick kiss and leave them to sleep, even if this involves a little crying. This is especially true between one and two years of age, when babies start becoming comfortable with sleeping on their own.

This doesn't mean it is wrong to cuddle or comfort your child before they sleep, just that it might help to find a balance that allows your child to learn to self-soothe and eventually sleep without needing quite so much parental input.

If your baby is still restless, instead of cuddling and fussing, stay in the room with them for a while and talk or sing to them. This will give them the comfort of your presence even if you aren't touching them.

> *Excessive 'active physical comforting' (for example, cuddling in arms) and reduced 'encouraging infant autonomy' (for example, leaving to cry) strategy use was associated with infant sleeping problems such as difficulty settling or waking five or more nights a week, waking three or more times a night, or waking for more than 20 minutes during the night.*

[J. Morrell & M. Cortina-Borja, 'The developmental change in strategies parents employ to settle young children to sleep, and their relationship to infant sleeping problems, as assessed by a new questionnaire: the Parental Interactive Bedtime Behaviour Scale', *Infant and Child Development,* *11* (1), 2002, pp. 17–41.]

## 21. Co-sleeping

In some cultures, co-sleeping with your infant, child, children or even extended family is considered not only practical, comfortable and cosy but virtually de rigueur.

However, in Western culture, we tend to think that all children should fall asleep independently, ideally in their own beds, in their own rooms with as little help from adults as possible, as early in life as possible.

At the same time, there is often an assumption that mum and dad should share a bed, even though the degree to which sleep quality is enhanced or undermined by this arrangement can be highly variable—the snorer, the blanket stealer, the late-night reader, the tosser and turner can all generate a lot more disturbance than any infant or child.

'Sleep problems' are amongst the most common and pressing problems encountered in paediatric practice in the Western world. However, in countries where co-sleeping is considered the done thing, reports of sleeping problems are virtually non-existent.

Parents who favour co-sleeping often report that any night-time wakings that do occur are not a problem since they are handled by immediate breastfeeding or soothing, resulting in a quick return to sleep for both babe and parents. Even parents who had not intended to co-sleep or for whom this was not the cultural norm often report finding that bringing their baby to bed is an easy and effective means of obtaining a good night's sleep.

It has been argued that solitary sleeping is vital for the development of children's independence. This is based on the assumption that if independence in sleep is achieved then children will be independent in other domains.

While anti-co-sleepers equate co-sleeping with excessive dependency, pro-co-sleepers say they choose and prefer to keep their little ones nearby through the night to nurture a sense of connectedness and security. The argument on the co-sleeping side is that co-sleeping promotes the development of secure infant-mother attachment, which in turn fosters competence and independence. As well as promoting closeness, co-sleeping has been shown to decrease children's night-time fears, nightmares and loneliness because of the constant soothing proximity of a parent.

Mothers of co-sleepers were found to be significantly more supportive of their children's autonomy, allowing them to make many decisions for themselves and exhibiting less harsh control, compared to mothers of solitary sleepers. Co-sleepers also tended to wean later than solitary sleepers, but there was no difference in terms of toilet training.

Of course, safety is paramount, so if you're co-sleeping with an infant or newborn it is vital to ensure safe bed-sharing practices to avoid smothering or increased risk of SIDS. Parents who co-sleep or bed-share should use a firm mattress, avoid waterbeds and sofas as sleeping surfaces, and take safety precautions to prevent the child slipping under doonas or being smothered by pillows, cushions or other accessories. Obviously, parents should never smoke or be under the influence of drugs or alcohol when in bed with their infant or child.

[Meret A. Keller & Wendy A. Goldberg, 'Co-sleeping: help or hindrance for young children's independence?' *Infant and Child Development*, 13, 2004, pp. 369–88.]

## 22. Continuity of care

Maternal sensitivity simply refers to a mother's ability to tune in to her child and respond in an appropriate way. Sensitive mothering includes being positive, supportive and emotionally available to the child, especially when the child is distressed. It's also about the *appropriateness* and *timing* of how mothers respond.

Children who experience sensitive and responsive mothering in infancy (particularly in the first twelve months) are expected to develop secure attachments which reflect confidence in Mum's emotional availability and responsiveness and promote a positive and trusting orientation towards the world in general. Some psychologists believe a secure attachment sets an individual up to be well-adjusted throughout life. It seems, however, that such views are overly simplistic and fail to take into account many other strong, influencing factors, including the fact that sensitive mothers with securely attached infants don't always remain as sensitive in their subsequent caregiving (and vice versa for insensitive mothers).

In one study, researchers looked at infant attachment to their mother at fifteen months of age as well as the sensitivity of mothering at two years of age, then compared developmental outcomes for these same children at age three.

While just over 50 per cent of women whose sensitive mothering in infancy produced securely attached babies continued to be sensitive in their mothering at two years, the remainder had become relatively insensitive.

Equally, while around half of the mothers whose caregiving of their baby was relatively insensitive remained so at two years old, the other half were assessed as having become more sensitive.

At three years of age the toddlers in the study were assessed for social competence, behaviour problems, school readiness and language development. While the kids who had both secure attachment and continuing sensitive mothering had the best developmental outcomes, and the kids with both insecure attachment and ongoing insensitive mothering did worst, a surprising picture emerged. Of the kids with an inconsistent history of attachment, the kids who had had insecure infant attachment as babies but were later more sensitively mothered did significantly better than kids who had had secure infant attachment but subsequently received insensitive parenting.

So it would seem infant attachment alone doesn't predict ongoing development, which is in fact shaped by both past and current experiences. If anything, later mothering has the greater bearing.

An interesting additional finding was that increased maternal stress—such as the death or illness of a relative or close friend, job loss, divorce or remarriage, financial difficulties, or depression—was associated with subsequent maternal insensitivity. Conversely, when insecurely attached infants later experienced more sensitive mothering, the mother was dealing with less stress than she'd experienced in the past.

So the good news is that no matter what life's been like up until now, what you do today and tomorrow may well have more impact than what you did in the past.

[Jay Belsky & R.M. Pasco Fearon, 'Early attachment security, subsequent maternal sensitivity, and later child development: does continuity in development depend upon continuity of caregiving?' *Attachment and Human Development*, vol. 4, no. 3, December 2002, pp. 361–87.]

## 23. Which parent are you?

Pick the animal that most describes you.

*Bonobos*: In these apes, everyone bows to the baby. The child is the most dominant member of the family and everyone is poised ready to grant their every wish and desire. 'Control' is what these parents call the remote for the television.

*Crocodiles*: These parents think life is boot camp. They control every facet of their children's lives but don't show much affection. Discipline, criticism and control are the family mantras. They are obsessively watchful and don't trust their children to do the right thing or to make the right decisions.

*Scorpions*: It's a little-known fact that scorpions actually eat their children. These parents often don't know how many children they have, much less where they are or if they are safe. They show no interest in their children's schooling or anything else.

*Ducks*: Clucky but no pushovers, these parents are controlling but not restrictive. They are highly involved in their children's lives and expect discipline and respect. They are constantly monitoring where their children are, who they are with, and what they are doing, but they also trust their children to make decisions. They have no problem putting their foot down, but they also encourage their children to be independent.

So how is your parenting style affecting your children's academic performance?

Bonobo children have high self-esteem, can focus

on problems and are active in solving them. But because everything is done for them and given to them, they tend not to be very motivated, or to want to do anything for themselves. They are so used to effortlessly being the centre of the universe that they don't feel they have to push themselves. Academically, bonobo children tend to be underachievers.

Crocodile children end up with a kind of learned helplessness where they can't do anything for themselves. The strict control of their parents takes the fun out of everything, and crocodile children are not very motivated. They are almost afraid to learn because they are so dependent on their parents, who discourage any kind of exploration or independent problem-solving.

Scorpion children are convinced they will fail at anything they try, so they don't try anything. Academically, they are a disaster. They have trouble focusing on projects and let other people boss them around.

Duck children rarely think about failure, and are assertive and determined problem solvers with good-self esteem. Academically, they are high performers, involved in school activities, and generally have a positive attitude.

So while it can be tempting to put your children at the centre of your universe, or make sure they resepct you by tightly controlling every fact of their lives, as usual a happy medium is best. If you're looking for animal inspiration go out and check out your nearest duck pond.

[K. Aunola, H.K. Stattin & J.E. Nurmi, 'Parenting styles and adolescents' achievement strategies', *Journal of Adolescence, 23* (2), 2000, pp. 205–22.]

## 24. Positive parenting

From as early as the age of three, children can display behaviours that indicate a predisposition to substance abuse, violence and delinquency. To some extent, aggression and fighting are a normal part of a child's development and can help kids learn to assert and defend themselves. However, persistent poorly controlled behaviour is a social handicap and augurs badly for a wide range of problems.

Kids who display high levels of antisocial behaviour often live with hostility and criticism from their parents as well as rejection by their peers. Along with frequently playing truant, most will leave school with no qualifications, and over a third will become recurrent juvenile offenders. In adulthood this offending usually continues, and they tend to have limited and unsatisfactory relationships and poor employment patterns.

Those at highest risk of such outcomes include kids who from very early on are defiant, aggressive and antisocial. Indeed kids with such conduct problems at a young age are three times more likely to have serious and chronic violent careers than those who begin antisocial behaviour later. The risk is further increased if these early onset conduct problems are met with harsh and inconsistent parenting, low parental monitoring and low parental involvement in school. If these early risk factors are not prevented or managed then these kids are at high risk of slipping over into a cascade of new problems, including academic failure, social exclusion, dropping out of school and joining with deviant peer groups, all of which further accelerate the liklihood of future violence.

The strong association between harsh, inconsistent parenting and antisocial behaviour in kids has long been noted, although initially it was unclear whether the parenting style was cause or consequence of the behaviour, or whether there might be an underlying genetic pre-disposition to such behaviour. Research has now shown that parents can indeed encourage antisocial behaviour by giving it attention while ignoring good, desirable, socially acceptable behaviour.

What can be done? Children of parents who were trained in 'positive parenting' showed significant improve-ments in their behaviour compared to kids whose parents receiveed no training. In one study, parents of problem kids aged three to eight underwent training in a group-based parenting program for around nine sessions. As a result their parenting style changed significantly, with greatly increased recognition of positive behaviour and no rewards (including attention) for negative behaviour.

As well as the hoped for significant reduction in conduct problems (such as defiance, aggression, fighting, violence and deviance) hyperactive symptoms were also significantly reduced. Kids with both inattention and hyperactivity difficulties responded to the parent training as well as kids without hyperactivity, suggesting that kids with a com-bination of behavioural problems as well as hyperactive and inattentive symptoms also benefit from positive parenting.

Given that aggressive behaviour in kids can 'crystallise' as early as age eight, making future learning and behavioural problems less responsive to treatment, nipping problems in the bud early is vital.

Positive parenting can be used as a preventive measure even before kids are diagnosed with defiant or conduct disorders, much as we immunise our kids from birth against a range of infectious diseases before they are contracted. Through learning more positive parenting techniques—giving positive attention to the good behaviours we want to encourage while minimising the attention we give to the behaviour we want to extinguish, rather than the other way round—we may be able to 'immunise' them against a range of serious behavioural problems.

So providing a safe, caring, nurturing environment with plenty of loving attention and affection is highly desirable. Parents need to be reasonable in their expectations and to enforce limits and boundaries. The first five years are crucial for setting the course of the rest of our kids' lives, but appropriate intervention is warranted at any age.

[Stephen Scott et al., 'Multicentre trial of positive parenting groups for childhood antisocial behaviour in clinical practice', *British Medical Journal*, 323.7306 (28 July 2001): 194.]

## 25. Kids are born helpful

Even the most patient, saintly parents occasionally wonder if their children are trying to drive them into a mental institution. This news should cheer you up: kids are born trying to help.

If you drop your keys by your feet and can't bend down to pick them up, chances are if a nearby child sees you they will immediately help you reach them. Researchers have found that even before kids can talk, they understand what you want—and they want to help you, even without being asked. Not only that, they will even help a complete stranger. The willingness to show kindness to strangers is one of our most cherished human qualities.

Since the instinct is already there, work with it. Ask them to help you pick toys up off the floor, put pegs in the washing basket, or bring you some chocolate. Virtues like these should be nurtured and encouraged.

*Researchers found that children as young as 18 months were helpful, before they could even speak or understand language. Children helped strangers in a variety of helping tasks, including obtaining objects out of reach, stacking books, and opening cabinet doors. The children did this repeatedly without praise or reward.*

[F. Warneken & M. Tomasello, 'Altruistic helping in human infants and young chimpanzees', *Science*, *311* (5765), 2006, pp. 1301–03.]

## 26. Mirror, mirror

We all want our children to be empathetic. Of course, even very young babies respond to emotion—a baby crying in the maternity ward can set off every other baby like a car alarm. But some empathy is more sophisticated than others. Like concern for the welfare of others, and understanding how your actions can have consequences for other people.

But if you are puzzled by your toddler's blank expression while you are crying your eyes out, or if questions like 'Do you want mummy to be upset?' seem to get nothing but blinking, try this little test.

Lightly dust a bit of blush on your child's nose, then show them a mirror. If your child reaches out to play with the funny baby with the red nose, they probably don't yet have any self-recognition. If they reach up to their own nose to get the blush off, then they are self-aware.

Around the age of two, toddlers start to recognise that they are the person in the mirror. They realise that they are different from everyone else, and they can experience emotions and feelings that other people don't share. But they also realise that they are the same as other people, and other people can feel what they are feeling, just at different times.

No one is exactly sure how this works, but all toddlers who show empathy can recognise themselves in mirrors. They are upset when someone else is upset, and can even get upset before they see the other person's reaction—for instance, if they see their sister's broken toy, they will be upset because they can *imagine* how she will feel when she sees it.

This is a trait that separates normal people from psychopaths. Psychopaths can intellectually understand that other people are upset, but they don't feel anything or want to do anything about it.

Like all good things, empathy takes time. So be patient.

[D. Bischof-Köhler, Empathy, Compassion and Cruelty, and How They Connect, paper presented at the Zivilisationsbruch mit Zuschauer, Gestalten des Mitgefühls, 2004.]

## 27. Be their Jiminy Cricket

When your kids reach about three, a whole range of interesting things start to happen. They become self-aware, they learn self-control, they get embarrassed, and they start considering what other people are thinking and feeling. It's as if they have a mental growth spurt in which they turn from pooping machines into real people.

But the most important change that takes place in their brains is that they start to develop a conscience. They begin to care about how other people feel, and realise that just because they are happy with the lovely lipstick mural they have drawn on the wall, it doesn't mean everyone else will be.

However, when you reprimand your child for something they have done, a slap on the wrist or other forms of punishment aren't enough. Children aren't puppies; you can't just rub their noses in the pee puddle then expect them to learn. Besides, you have a wonderful tool at your disposal to teach your children the difference between right and wrong—language.

Mothers who explain the *emotional* consequences of their child's actions—for example, how it makes her feel *angry* to see her nice clean wall covered in lipstick and how *sad* she is that it will take her all of Saturday to clean it off—have children who are more likely to feel guilty over their actions, and feel sorrow they have hurt someone else.

So like Jiminy says, they should always let their conscience be their guide. But sometimes they might need a little help from you.

*The daily conversations a child shares with parents are often imbued with messages about social and moral issues, as well as references to feelings. Emotion-laden discourse by the mother was related to multiple dimensions of a child's early conscience development. Mothers who made frequent references to feelings and moral evaluatives had children who showed more behavioural internalization and were more likely to express guilt after wrongdoing.*

[D.J. Laible & R.A. Thompson, 'Mother–child discourse, attachment security, shared positive affect, and early conscience development', *Child Development*, *71* (5), 2000, pp. 1424–40.]

## 28. Velcro magic

It must be tough to be a baby—all those interesting objects and no muscular strength to pick them up. You can help. Get some velcro and either sew or stick it onto some mittens. Then get some toys that stick to the velcro. As your baby lies in their cot, they will experience velcro magic!

It may sound like a bizarre thing to do, but creating these 'sticky mittens' actually improves your baby's exploration skills, and allows them to engage more with objects, which is important because they learn more quickly about their environment as their visual and oral skills develop. They'll also become more interested in objects, which will help with everything from building blocks to puzzles, to number games.

*Infants who gained experience in the use of 'sticky mittens' showed more object engagement via a number of measures, and showed more sophisticated object exploration strategies compared to their inexperienced peers. The results suggest that the early simulated experience reaching for objects serves to jump-start the process of object engagement in young infants. The mittens experience may also have had an indirect effect on fine motor skills.*

[A. Needham, T. Barrett & K. Peterman, 'A pick-me-up for infants' exploratory skills: early simulated experiences reaching for objects using sticky mittens enhances young infants' object exploration skills', *Infant Behavior and Development, 25* (3), 2002, pp. 279–95.]

## 29. It's never too early to start reading

Before children even open their mouths to say 'Mama' for the first time, they are absorbing sounds around them and figuring out how to turn them into words.

Reading to your children daily, or at least several times a week, when they are as young as fourteen months old improves vocabulary and comprehension. When they hit the age of two, reading improves not only their cognitive skills but also sensory skills, memory, problem-solving and the ability to understand mathematical concepts.

Reading to your children three to six times a week is likely to give them a better vocabulary than children who are only read to once or twice a week. Reading daily has even more advantages such as improving vocabulary, memory and problem solving. These improvements are consistent no matter how rich or poor you are.

The reading ability of children before they start school predicts how good their literacy levels are at age seven. So give them a headstart,with lots of books before bedtime.

[B.R. Oliver, P.S. Dale & R. Plomin, 'Predicting literacy at age 7 from preliteracy at age 4', *Psychological Science, 16* (11), 2005, pp. 861–65. H. Raikes, et al., 'Mother–child bookreading in low-income families: correlates and outcomes during the first three years of life', *Child Development, 77* (4), 2006, pp. 924–53.]

## 30. *Baby Einstein* sucks

It's your dream come true. Park your baby in front of the television, put on an educational DVD, and do the laundry, your taxes or the million other things on your list while your baby absorbs the alphabet, simple mathematics and charming songs.

The problem with so-called 'learning while watching' programs is that they don't work. Not only that, they retard your child's language development. For every hour spent watching these programs, babies between eight and sixteen months old actually learn six to eight *fewer* words than babies who don't watch them. From seventeen to twenty-four months, the effect is neutral—infants' language isn't harmed, but they aren't learning anything either.

For the first three years, your baby's brain develops extremely rapidly. Educational DVDs may be entertaining but they have limited language, short scenes and flashy images that probably lead to mental modelling that impedes vocabulary learning. And the more time they spend in front of the television, the less time they spend with you.

The only thing *Baby Einstein*, *Brainy Baby* and (we hate to say it because we love it) *Sesame Street* are producing is a generation of overstimulated children who will have short attention spans once they hit preschool.

When kids turn two it's a different story, and our beloved *Sesame Street* can help toddlers learn numbers and their ABCs. But babies learn best from real people like you and your family, not cartoon people or Muppets on a television screen. (Don't think that you sitting in front of the box with them helps, either—parents watching with the kids did nothing to improve their scores.)

So take the 60 bucks you might spend on *Baby Einstein* and hire a cleaner instead. The extra time you spend talking to your baby will make more of a difference than those four bouncy Wiggles ever could.

[F. Zimmerman, D. Christakis & A. Meltzoff. 'Associations between media viewing and language development in children under age 2 years,' *The Journal of Pediatrics, 151* (4), 2007, pp. 364–8.]

## 31. When to teach them a foreign language

Are you one of the lucky people who speaks more than one language? Perhaps your father is Greek, or your mother is Chinese. Do you want your children to learn that language too, but you don't want it to interfere with their English? When is the best time to teach them?

The answer is as soon as they are born. For the first six months, babies are especially capable of recognising the varied tones and sounds of different languages. From six to twelve months this ability declines sharply. So it's actually easier for children to learn a foreign language when they are younger than older.

Many parents are worried that their children will somehow get confused and start talking a mixed language. But children's brains are incredibly plastic and, after many years of debate, there is evidence that children who learn two languages don't learn any more slowly than children with only one language. If they do mix languages, it's probably in a similar way to how their parents or grandparents do.

For those of us who don't speak another language but were putting our hopes in those foreign language DVDs, forget it. Children who watch educational programs designed to teach a foreign language, like Mandarin, learn no more Mandarin than children who don't watch the programs at all. Even with the close-up of the nice lady's face looking right at your little one, and a professional sound system, it doesn't make a difference. They might pick up some vocabulary, but they can't grasp the pronunciation and the grammar.

Children need a real human being to learn a different language. So send them to Grandma or Grandpa or hire a foreign nanny. Otherwise, plain old English will have to do.

[L.A. Petitto, et al., 'Bilingual signed and spoken language acquisition from birth: implications for the mechanisms underlying early bilingual language acquisition', *Journal of Child Language, 28* (02), 2001, pp. 453–96.]

## 32. Going to Granny's

We all want our children to bloom in their ability to think and use language, and research has shown that quality care in infancy and early childhood, whether provided by a parent or someone else, enhances this.

Features of adult–child interactions that represent what is considered good caregiving include: sensitivity and responsiveness to the child's needs and signals, positive affect (such as being bright, happy and encouraging), frequent verbal and social interaction (in other words, being chatty, friendly and involving) and cognitive stimulation (provoking and sustaining the child's interest in things that provide food for thought and exploration).

One study compared outcomes in terms of cognitive and language performance and ability for youngsters at 15, 24 and 36 months who had had different types of care in infancy and early childhood: some had exclusively (or virtually so) maternal care for the first three years of life, others had varying amounts of care in a childcare centre setting, and the rest had home-based care (family daycare or care at home by a carer or relative other than the mother, such as a grandparent or father).

Consistent with other research, children in childcare centres did better than children in home-based child care. The advantages of centre-based over home-based child care may be that children in centres are exposed to a more diverse range of language models, a richer language environment and more opportunities to encounter stimulating materials and events than children in less formal settings. Also, children in childcare centres are more likely than children in home-based child care to be exposed to a sizeable group of same-age peers, and the group setting may make more demands on children to use language to meet their needs.

Of course, the quality of the childcare centre is crucial to this, with the best environment for cognitive and language development being a childcare centre with a high level of sensitive and linguistically stimulating care.

The results also showed that while the quality of the home environment, family background (such as maternal vocabulary and family income) and the quality of the mother's interactions with her child were highly predictive of children's outcomes, children looked after exclusively by their mums for the first three years of life (ten or less hours per week of non-maternal care was still counted as exclusive maternal care) had similar scores for cognitive and language development to children in non-maternal child care.

The only differences were that children in exclusive maternal care did not do as well as children in medium to high-quality child care for language (vocabulary production and sentence complexity) at 24 months, but did better than children in low-quality care for verbal comprehension at 36 months of age.

Overall, children in a formal childcare or preschool setting had better cognitive and language skills than children in all other types of care at 36 months. Quality of care (as measured by levels of responsiveness and sensitivity in caregiving, as well as frequency and quality of language stimulation) during the first two years of life consistently predicted cognitive and language performance. The number of hours spent in child care bore no consistent relation to cognitive or language development. So, more time in high-quality care was not found to be related to more advanced cognitive or language development than less time in high-quality care, suggesting that earlier or more child care in itself is neither particularly good nor bad for children's cognitive or language development.

So there you have it: in terms of cognitive and language development, exclusive (or virtually exclusive) maternal care is not necessarily better than good quality centre-based child care, and good quality centre-based child care is better than home-based child care with a non-maternal carer (related or not), even when the caregiver ratings and frequency of caregiver–child verbal interactions are comparable. They might not get as many rock cakes, but children actually do better in childcare centres than with Grandma.

[National Institute of Child Health and Human Development Early Child Care Research Network, 'The relation of child care to cognitive and language development', *Child Development*, vol. 71, No. 4, July/August 2000, pp. 960–80.]

## 33. Mum care versus child care

In debates about child care, little attention has been given to what the quality of care at home would be if the child were there all day with their mum.

While the devotion of a sensitive, attentive mother who is well supported by a loving, financially solvent spouse and a collaborative and harmonious social network is considered by many to be the ideal—especially for children under the age of twelve months—parental stress, lack of support, lack of experience and/or lack of knowledge may well make formal childcare a more desirable option, at least for some of the time.

This is reflected in a recent study which showed that for children receiving optimal parenting, attachment security (whether the child was securely attached to their mum, or whether the attachment was insecure or avoidant) decreased with the more hours they spent in childcare per week. Conversely, for children receiving less optimal parenting, increased hours in child care actually resulted in improved attachment security.

So it's clearly not a case of 'less is more' for all. For some parents, spending more time apart actually improves bonding and attachment with their child. This may be because the child becomes more sociable as a result of their time at child care and their parents in turn respond more favourably to them, or perhaps it's because the childcare providers encourage more effective parenting skills, essentially acting as parental coaches, setting examples of appropriate child-rearing practices, providing guidelines for age-appropriate expectations, and sharing information on child development.

Or perhaps simply by giving mums a break from the responsibility of child-rearing, letting them develop other facets of their lives, providing access to other women in the same boat and relieving some parental stress, child care allows parents to enjoy the time that they spend with their children more. Surely there's nothing wrong with that?

[Yvonne M. Caldera & Sybil Hart, 'Exposure to childcare, parenting style and attachment security', *Infant and Child Development*, vol. 13, 2004, pp. 21–33.]

## 34. Yes, please

Here's a little fact you can have a lot of fun with—and it may even improve your parenting experience exponentially. Until children are two years old, they say 'yes' to almost all 'yes or no' questions.

Answering a question is actually quite complicated. First, you have to understand the words the person is saying. Then you have to understand the grammar. Then you have to understand enough about your culture to know the socially acceptable answer. (We all know the correct answer to 'Do I look fat in this dress?'.)

Young children have what is called a 'yes bias'. Regardless of the question, they just say 'yes'. You could ask them 'Did you just smear lipstick all over Mummy's wall?' and they will solemnly nod their head, even if it was really that nasty child from next door—so be careful of how you phrase your questions when you are trying to gather information.

We suggest going crazy with questions such as 'Is Mummy the most beautiful woman in the world?' and 'Will you buy Daddy a villa in Tuscany when you grow up?'

Enjoy it while it lasts. The 'yes bias' runs out when they turn three.

[V. Heather Fritzley & K. Lee, 'Do young children always say yes to yes—no questions? A metadevelopmental study of the affirmation bias,' *Child Development, 74* (5), 2003, pp. 1297–313.]

## 35. Coping with stress and the one-way domino effect

Feeling unhappy at work can lead to an increase in a person's overall stress levels, which in turn sees people with children showing less warmth towards them. So it's not surprising to hear that adolescents with stressed parents exhibit higher levels of problem behaviour and conflict with their parents.

What isn't widely known is that women tend to be responsive to their partners' work stress in ways that are not necessarily reciprocated by their partner, and this is regardless of which spouse is working the longer hours. So not only do a father's stress levels impact on his kids but also on his partner.

Perhaps this is because, in general, even when a woman is working full time, her partner's income is often greater and he is seen as the primary economic provider, giving his work more visibility and status in the family. It could also be that women simply have to move on from the stresses of the workday to deal with their household and childcare responsibilities and are therefore less likely to pass work-related stress on to their spouse. Men show a larger autonomic nervous system response to stress, and recover more slowly than women. This means men are also more likely to carry work stress home for their partner to notice and react to.

Researchers have found that spousal interactions are significantly improved when women allow their partner to withdraw from family interactions after a particularly stressful work day. Indeed, in the short term this withdrawal from the family can be an adaptive response to high-level work stress—if you have the luxury of being able to withdraw.

Working mothers suffering work stress tend to want to withdraw from both positive and negative interactions with their kids on high-stress days, but this is not always possible. Not surprisingly, on days when both parents experience work and home stress, parent–adolescent tensions escalate.

The tendency for daily stresses to impact on the family and lead to tense parent–child interactions was more pronounced in families where the mother worked full time. This may be because mothers working less hours have more time and energy to manage both their own emotions and deal with the family's.

A study of single mothers found that women were less likely to transmit anxious feelings to their adolescent kids if they had some time alone. Interestingly, social support didn't seem to help, only time by themselves.

While withdrawal from family interactions might help in the short term, repeated removal of oneself because of chronic work stress can lead to the parent being seen as inaccessible and disengaged. This has a negative impact on their ability to parent, with children escalating their bids for attention and partners protesting and pushing for change.

So if you or your partner have stressful workplaces, it's important to try to recognise the stress your job creates and the impact it has on your emotional responses and interactions with your spouse and children. And if you or your partner are suffering chronically high levels of work stress it's worth talking to healthcare professionals and family members about strategies to cope with stress and minimise its potentially corrosive effects on your family.

[Ann C. Crouter and Matthew F. Bumpus, 'Linking parents' work stress to children's and adolescents' psychological adjustment', *Current Directions in Psychological Science*, vol. 10, no. 5, October 2001, pp. 156–9.]

## 36. Fathers and sons

Most modern-day fathers spend more time with their sons than their daughters, and not just when their sons get older and can chuck a football around. Men tend to be more available to their sons and perform more caregiving tasks with their sons than daughters from babyhood on. Of course, this has the tendency to stop if the male child is the difficult, screaming, crying type, in which case Dad is more than happy to pass the baby back to Mum.

According to human capital theory, the parent who works longer hours and/or brings in more income to the household should be involved in fewer household and caregiving tasks, but the fact is that even when both parents work full time, mothers still tend to spend far more time with their kids than fathers. Dads may disagree, but this is probably because fathers tend to consider themselves present and available when they are at home, even if they're checking emails at the other end of the house. Mothers only count face-to-face time with their children.

And even when dads do pitch in, it can lead to conflict if they don't really want to engage in the caregiving tasks but are forced to because their partner simply cannot manage everything from work to household tasks to dealing with the kids. This is consistent with 'gender-ideology theory', whereby a parent's own internal conflict over appropriate or 'natural' gender roles leads to conflict between parents.

Western society still has a long way to go before there is true equality between the sexes on the home front. In the meantime, if you're a dad, try to balance the time you spend with your sons and daughters and avoid the temptation to avoid your little boy if he is difficult, fussy, crying or hard-to-soothe. There's more to fatherhood than just tossing a ball around.

If you're a mum, remember that having a career doesn't necessarily mean you will do an equal share of the housework or caregiving! 'Having it all' still often means 'doing it all', and when your partner does help out it may come at a price. If you want someone to help with the housework and the kids, and you can afford it, we highly recommend a dishwasher, a cleaner and an occasional babysitter.

[Elizabeth E. Manlove & Lynne Vernon-Feagans, 'Caring for infant daughters and sons in dual-earner households: Maternal reports of father involvement in weekday time and tasks', *Infant and Child Development*, vol. 11, 2002, pp. 305–20.]

## 37. Sugar and spice, slugs and snails

Boys will be boys and girls will play with Barbies and imagine being fairy princesses and little mummies . . . or so the story goes. But are these stereotypes created by the world we live in, or is it all in the genes?

Kids' preferences for certain toys are striking from as early as age one, and by the time they're three girls will typically be deeply into doll's, doll's houses, tea sets and other accoutrements of domestic bliss, while boys are shooting, racing, firing, smashing, exploding and otherwise creating chaos with guns, swords, cars, trains, trucks, rockets and jet planes. And current research shows that the girliest toddler girls will just get more and more girly, and the most machismo-infused toddler boys will simply become even more rugged and gnarly over time.

It's not just toys that children have a gender preference for. Girls prefer to play with girls and boys with boys from as early as two to three years old, irrespective of nationality, culture or who their parents think they should play with. Even when kids are not with adults they will tend to play with kids of their own sex, especially when they are with kids of similar age. And this tendency increases with age. At four and a half, kids play with same-sex peers three times more than with opposite-sex peers; by six and a half this has increased to ten times as much. Active avoidance of playmates of the opposite sex is also common.

It's in their behaviour, too. From age three, boys tend to engage in more active, rough and tumble play while girls talk to each other more and are more socially nurturing. In turn, girls' aggression, when present, is more likely to be relationship-damaging behaviour such as excluding a certain girl or girls from a social circle. From as early as age three, boys will be inclined to use force to sort out their differences while girls tend towards compromise. In terms of pretend play, boys act out heroic roles involving fighting or adventure while girls dress up in feminine clothes and enact family characters and domestic scenes.

These patterns continue into the early school years where boys prefer playing in large packs with other boys while girls tend to congregate with one or two other girls. While girls' friendships tend to be characterised by emotional and physical closeness, boys' are founded more on shared activities and interests.

It seems the processes influencing sex-typing have a tendency to compound and multiply their effects. A recent study found boys with the most masculine behaviour at two and a half had significantly more of an increase in sex-typed behaviour by the ages of five and eight than less masculine boys. Similarly, girls who initially displayed the most feminine characteristics became more markedly feminine over the years from age two and a half to eight.

The major factors behind such sex-typed differences are thought to be biology (including early hormonal influences), social learning and cognitive developmental processes, along with the interplay between all three.

However, while hormonal factors account at least for the onset of behavioural preferences, there is little evidence that they play a role in the increase in sex-typed behaviour as children get older. However, social learning and cognitive developmental studies have shown that playing with same-sex peers directly increases sex-typed behaviour over and above individual tendencies to do so, especially amongst girls.

So if your daughter's favourite outfit is a pink tutu and she shares intimate secrets with her similarly garbed bestie, doing her best to avoid being shot at by her slingshot-toting brother and his ruffian mates, generally the differences between siblings are only going to become more pronounced as they get older.

By all means encourage and be open to diversity. Just be aware that a lot of the foundations for what you are seeing were laid down in the womb, subject to the prevailing hormonal conditions. And once they're on the path they're on, it may well become a self-fulfilling prophecy.

If, on the other hand, you have a tomboy daughter or a gentler, pearls-and-lace loving son, there's no need to worry. But don't necessarily assume they are going to change too much. Certainly exposure to sex-typed role models, same-sex peers and sex-typed activities may enhance their own sex-typed characteristics if that's what you want, however if they are not that way inclined it may be difficult to force them into such activities in the first place.

Boys will be boys, but some boys will be hairdressers, fashion designers and make-up artists. Of course sex-typed behaviour does not equate to sexuality—that's a whole different topic.

[Susan Golombok et al., 'Developmental trajectories of sex-typed behaviour in boys and girls: A longitudinal general population study of children aged 2.5–8 Years', *Child Development*, vol. 79, no. 5, Sept/Oct 2008, pp. 1583–93.]

## 38. The battle of wills

They don't call it the 'terrible twos' for nothing. At the same time that toddlers start to develop a will of their own, you have to start imposing your will on them. This, not surprisingly, is going to lead to conflict.

As frustrating as it is to have your judgment questioned by a two-year-old, especially one who eats their own snot, try not to resort to a snappy 'because I said so'. While it seems perfectly obvious to you that lying face down and screaming at the top of your lungs is an unacceptable way to ask for a chocolate bar, it may not be that obvious to your child.

Similar clashes between parents and young children have been noted to occur up to fifteen times an hour—exhausting by anyone's standards. Fighting may not be much fun at the time, but you can turn it into an important learning tool.

As a parent, your emotions and your reaction to your child's emotions shape the development of the child's emotional understanding. The way you explain yourself when you do something, like take away a sharp object, will help them understand your perspective and the issues raised in the conflict. This, in turn, will shape the way they deal with conflict in other situations, and increase their ability to put themselves in someone else's shoes.

For instance, 'I'm worried about you with that knife, darling—I need to take it away because I would be so upset if you hurt yourself' is better than, 'Give me that knife, you stupid child, before I stab you with it myself!'

Try to explain yourself calmly. Justify your actions, and tell them how you are feeling and why. Though they may not like the outcome, at least they know you have their best interests at heart.

[D.J. Laible & R.A. Thompson, 'Mother–child conflict in the toddler years: lessons in emotion, morality, and relationships', *Child Development*, 73 (4), 2002, pp. 1187–203.]

## 39. Are we normal?

Raising toddlers can be challenging, even when they're seemingly healthy and developmentally normal. Compared to five year olds, for example, toddlers and infants simply make more frequent and more intense demands on parents. But what is 'normal'?

A recent study looked at families with youngsters from age nine months to three years. The subjects were predominantly in upper middle class, two-parent families, where the parents had a tertiary level of education and lived in relatively homogeneous, highly affluent suburbs. Nearly a quarter of the parents reported their kids exhibited twelve or more of the following behaviours.

| Toddler behaviour | Percentage of parents who reported problems with this behaviour |
|---|---|
| whining | 43% |
| refusing to obey instructions unless threatened | 37% |
| getting angry when not allowed to have their own way | 35% |
| refusing to eat the food with which they are presented | 33% |
| acting defiant | 30% |
| interrupting | 30% |
| dawdling getting dressed | 29% |
| temper tantrums | 29% |
| refusal to go to bed on time | 29% |

| | |
|---|---|
| slowness in getting ready for bed | 24% |
| refusing to obey rules | 24% |
| refusing to do chores | 24% |
| having difficulty entertaining themselves | 22% |
| yelling or screaming | 20% |
| constantly seeking attention | 20% |
| hitting parents | 20% |
| crying too easily | 20% |
| teasing other kids | 18% |
| arguing with parents about rules | 18% |
| verbally fighting with siblings | 18% |
| verbally impertinent with parents | 17% |
| physically fighting with siblings | 15% |
| lying | 11% |
| destroying toys | 9% |
| wetting the bed | 7% |
| stealing | 1% |

Sound familiar? If so, you're probably quite normal, and so are your kids.

Still, even if we accept that each of these annoying behaviours in isolation may be normal at this age, the additive effect of such frequent and intense demands and aggravations for any parent, particularly the primary carer, can have a big impact on their ability to cope.

Interestingly, while 60 per cent of the mothers surveyed were employed, they all reported similar levels of difficulties and needs for help with child-rearing irrespective of whether they worked outside the home or not.

No wonder mothers' groups are so popular, especially for mums with kids under three. It certainly helps to gather in packs to discuss the latest things your children have concocted to drive you crazy, and it helps to know that almost everyone else has some cross to bear and that, if anything, you might be getting off easy.

If what you are describing seems off the scale though—for example, instead of saying 'Same here!' and then regaling you with similar tales, the other mothers are wide-eyed with mouths agape—by all means seek professional medical advice. Otherwise, sit back and listen to your fellow mums' torrid tales of two-year-old-inflicted torture and count yourself lucky that your little devil(s) are not quite as devilish as some of your mothers' group mates'. In fact, maybe in comparison they're little angels and you're doing one hell of a heavenly job.

[Marion O'Brien, 'Child-rearing difficulties reported by parents of infants and toddlers,' *Journal of Pediatric Psychology*, vol. 21, no. 3, 1996, pp. 433–46.]

## 40. Dealing with temper tantrums

Of course not all two year old behaviour is terrible—some is terrific—but it can be an age that brings with it disruptive behaviour, including those raging temper tantrums. While this peak of pique in early toddlerdom usually settles down during the preschool years and—thankfully—dissipates almost completely by the time kids start school, there are parents for whom the 'Terrible Twos' are succeeded by the 'Thrashing Threes', the 'Formidable Fours', the 'Fearsome Fives' and the 'Sixes that Totally Suck' . . . all the way to the 'Torturous Teens' and beyond.

So what factors govern which path your child will follow? And what role do parents play? How early can risk factors for chronic disruptive behaviour problems be identified and, most importantly, is it possible to prevent disruptive kids from turning into antisocial adolescents and adults?

One of the factors that can lead to disruptive behaviour continuing beyond toddlerdom and the preschool years is temperament. Temperament includes how an individual reacts to their environment (reactivity) as well as their ability to regulate these reactions (regulation). The good news (or bad, depending on what your toddler is like) is that a child's emotional and physical reactivity during a meltdown is, by and large, considered a fairly stable and enduring aspect of their temperament.

Normally as kids grow up they learn how to regulate their emotions and behaviour in a variety of contexts, leading eventually to positive social skills and less disruptive behaviour. Kids who are prone to frustration and have limited regulatory skills, however, may well develop negative social behaviour, and lower social competence, with a greater likelihood of being defiant, aggressive, non-compliant, antisocial and having poor impulse control.

But it's not all pre-determined. Another factor affecting kids' levels of frustration, emotional regulation and socially appropriate behaviour is how their mother responds, behaves and interacts with them. Kids learn to manage their own distress and behaviour through the complex social interactions they have with their primary caregiver. Controlling, harsh or rejecting behaviour from parents is associated with aggression, non-compliance and a whole range of other behavioural problems in their kids. Indeed, hostile or intrusive mums may worsen their kids' frustration and poor regulatory skills, resulting in even more severe disruptive behaviour. But does that mean a high level of parental control is always a bad thing?

One study followed kids from age two to five, looking at their levels of disruptive behaviour in relation to such potential contributing factors as how they reacted to frustration, their ability to regulate emotions and how much maternal control was exerted. Results showed that kids with high levels of disruptive behaviour, reaching seriously problematic levels at age five, were most likely to have a combination of high reactivity and high maternal control or low self-regulation and low maternal control. That is, while parents being very controlling may cause disruptive behaviour to escalate in highly reactive kids, less regulated kids may well need the additional structure and direction from their parents to curtail disruptive behaviour.

It seems one size does not fit all. A child may be wayward or misbehaving in spite of, or indeed because of, a strict, highly controlling parent. So how do you know which you've got and how to deal with them?

Sensitive parenting means tailoring your response to the individual child, observing their reactions and adjusting your subsequent responses accordingly. If your child is quick to get worked up and become emotionally distressed by frustration, then controlling behaviour may increase their frustration and make their behaviour worse. On the other hand, if your child has difficulty settling down and regulating those excited or tumultuous emotions, providing some structure and direction may help them decrease their bad behaviour.

Of course if disruptive behaviour continues to escalate despite your best efforts, it may be worthwhile seeking professional advice, just to make sure that what you're currently doing is not in fact making things worse, and to find out if there is an underlying issue that needs to be addressed.

[Kathryn A. Degnan et al., 'Profiles of disruptive behaviour across early childhood: contributions of frustration reactivity, physiological regulation and maternal behaviour', *Child Development*, vol. 79, no. 5, Sept/Oct 2008 pp. 1357–76.]

## 41. It was an accident

'You did that on purpose!' is usually delivered in a high-pitched whine that can make any parent grind their teeth in frustration, especially if it isn't true. But as annoying as these kinds of accusations are, they show an important milestone in children's morality. It means that your kids are starting to know the difference between something bad that happens by accident (you run over their toy in the driveway) and something bad that someone does deliberately (you confiscate a toy as punishment).

Kids develop this ability around three years of age, which is also when they can start saying they did something by accident when in fact they did it on purpose. It's an ideal time to start talking to them about right and wrong. Intent is a large part of the crime. So even though they might be angry at parents who run over toys in the driveway, they know you didn't mean it and can work on another very important skill—forgiveness.

[A.M. Leslie, J. Knobe & A. Cohen, 'Acting intentionally and the side-effect effect', *Psychological Science, 17* (5), 2006, pp. 421–7. M. Siegal, & C.C. Peterson, 'Preschoolers' understanding of lies and innocent and negligent mistakes', *Developmental Psychology, 34* (2), 1998, pp. 332–41.]

## 42. To smack or not to smack

Now who can honestly say that at some point in the life of their child they haven't wanted to give them a good slap and send them to their room?

Well you're not alone. Up to 95 per cent of toddlers have experienced some sort of physical discipline, be it hitting, slapping, spanking, or the like. Fortunately such actions rarely escalate into abuse. Furthermore it is believed that only the more extreme forms of physical punishment have consistently negative effects on a child's development, with typical spankings having little lasting impact on their well-being. However, if corporal punishment is administered too severely or too frequently it becomes abuse.

There is little doubt that children who witness abusive relationships and domestic violence do suffer as a result. Mounting research shows associations between domestic violence and children's maladjustment, with children from violent households twice as likely to have clinical behavioural problems as children from non-violent homes.

And the most likely cause of such violence is parental stress, that is, a parent's belief that they are ill-equipped or unable to deal with the daily hassles and accumulated minor stresses associated with their caregiver role. Basically, all those typical yet frustrating and annoying or distressing demands mount up to create even higher levels of parental stress and a perception that they are simply unable to cope. Such parents tend to view their kids' behaviour in a more negative light and are more likely to use physical discipline.

It makes sense that anything that can help alleviate parental stress and reduce family violence and the use of physical discipline is in a child's best interest. Formal child care can give parents the break they need, reducing caregiving demands, parental stress and consequently the use of physical discipline. Childcarers and associated social networks can also provide an important form of support, as well as shaping parents' disciplinary norms, by promoting positive-parenting practices and providing information about children's developmental needs. The childcare environment can also give parents the opportunity to connect with other parents in the community.

Childcare providers can play an important role too, monitoring children's well-being, keeping note of their health and physical condition and potentially reporting suspected abuse. Even the knowledge that such caregivers are in regular contact with their kids may deter some parents from using physical discipline that could be construed as abusive.

Domestic violence (assessed in one study by asking whether couples ended up hitting or throwing things at each other when arguing) was more frequent amongst parents who reported using physical discipline with their children or who endorsed its use in a hypothetical situation (saying they would spank if their child got angry and hit them).

Lower income, low-education and single-parent families had higher rates of smacking, and lower income, low-education parents were more likely to report having experienced violent arguments with their partner. Parenting stress was also higher for these disadvantaged groups.

Early education and formal childcare programs were found to have a protective effect, reducing parents' use of physical discipline and resulting in less domestic violence, especially within lower income families.

[Katherine A. Magnuson & Jane Waldfogel, 'Preschool child care and parents' use of physical discipline', *Infant and Child Development*, vol. 14, 2005, pp. 177–98.]

## 43. One way to prevent obesity

We are going to let you in on one of life's great mysteries: why it's tough to lose weight on a diet (and keep it off). We've all been there—after being good all week (nothing but salads and grilled chicken), by some tragic accident you come face to face with a brownie. It's been heated in the oven, so the outside is crispy while the inside is gooey and soft. Next to the brownie are two scoops of creamy vanilla ice cream.

There goes the diet.

The combination of dietary restraint (trying not to eat food that makes you fat) and disinhibition (the hopelessness you feel when confronted with a brownie) make losing weight extremely difficult.

What does this have to do with your kids?

Children with parents who deprive themselves of food, then cave in and binge, are more likely to develop the same patterns and become obese. So don't talk constantly about which foods make you fat or be obsessive about your children's diet. Make sure you have healthy food available, and set a good example with the food you eat. But what's life without the occasional brownie?

[M. Y Hood et al., 'Parental eating attitudes and the development of obesity in children, *The Framingham Children's Study*', 24 (10), 2000.]

## 44. Forbidden fruit

Attempts by parents to restrict young girls' access to 'yummy' foods such as chocolate, chips, ice cream and lollies can actually have the opposite effect, while generating feelings of guilt and shame around the consumption of those foods.

Naturally parents need to be responsible and sensible about the types of food they make available to their kids and the amounts that they consume, but taking an excessively restrictive approach can have unintended effects. Being overly controlling of their food choices limits their opportunities to practise self-control and, in turn, their ability to self-regulate their food needs. Indeed, in research conducted on preschool children it was found that the more restrictive the parents, the more the kids tended to overeat and become overweight, even at preschool age.

Self-imposed restrictive eating practices and draconian diets can have a negative effect on an adult's psychological well-being, self-esteem and physical self-appraisal. With kids, parental use of such restriction also has negative psychological effects as they unwittingly learn to associate eating 'bad' foods with a sense of guilt or shame, as well as a sense that they cannot control themselves or trust their own instincts around food.

In a recent study, parents and girls (aged four to six) described the degree to which certain foods were restricted, limited or monitored in their family. Was it allowed at all? If so, when and how much? Would the parent be upset if the child ate it without asking? Was it kept out of reach or kept out of the house altogether? How often could the child have it relative to how often she asked for it? The girls were questioned regarding whether their parents let them have such foods and whether they were 'anytime, snack, dessert or special-time foods'.

After eating a standard lunch of bread, meat, cheese, apple sauce, carrots, biscuits and milk, each girl was given access to play with a number of toys. At the same time, generous portions of snack foods (such as chocolate, ice cream, popcorn, chips, lollies, choc-chip biscuits, nuts, pretzels, fig bars, and frozen yoghurt) were made available. Each child was told that she could play with any of the toys and eat any of the foods while the experimenter was out of the room for ten minutes.

Afterwards the girls were asked how much they had eaten and how they felt about it: did they feel they'd eaten too much? Did they feel sad, happy, okay, guilty or ashamed about this? How would they feel if Mum or Dad found out what they had eaten?

The most consumed snacks were chocolate, lollies, chips and ice cream, with the girls having anywhere between none and 436 kilocalories. For any given snack food, between 11 and 23 per cent of girls reported a sense of having eaten too much and feeling bad (guilty or ashamed) about eating it. Overall, 50 per cent of the girls reported eating 'too much', 44 per cent felt guilty about eating at least one or more of the foods, 30 per cent said they would feel bad if their mum found out, and 37 per cent would feel bad if their dad found out what they had eaten.

The girls' guilt and shame were a direct reflection of their belief that they would not normally be allowed to have those foods. Their perception of having eaten 'too much' was not related to the actual amount they ate so much as whether they thought their parents would have let them have the food.

Previous research has found that many kids report feelings of guilt about eating foods that might make them fat and it is thought that these negative feelings originate at least in part from parental expectations that they should restrict their food intake, particularly of 'yummy' foods. Girls who regularly had access to 'yummy' foods ate the least, and girls for whom it was forbidden gorged the most.

Fostering healthy eating habits should focus on providing variety and promoting moderation and the enjoyment of food rather than outright restriction of any particular foods.

While it is natural for parents to wish to promote healthy eating habits, it is important to be aware that an overly restrictive approach may have the converse effect of promoting intake of the very foods you wanted to limit. Efforts aimed at fostering healthy eating habits should *not* focus on restricting kids' intake of palatable, energy-dense foods so much as providing variety and promoting moderation. Ideally parents and caregivers should aim to create a flexible yet structured eating environment where kids are encouraged to make their own reasonable decisions about what and how much to eat.

[Jennifer O. Fisher et al., 'Parents' restrictive feeding practices are associated with young girls' negative self-evaluation of eating', *Journal of the American Dietetic Association*, vol. 100, no. 11, November 2000, pp. 1341–46.]

## 45. The upside of sugar

A lot of things combine to shape our views about diet, health and well-being. It seems like every other day someone is telling us what's good for us to eat, from the importance of breakfast to the evils of snacking, sugar and food additives, and the benefits or otherwise of vitamin supplements.

If what you're doing is working for you, and you and your brood are in effortlessly tiptop health, then keep going with it. However, you might like to know what the science boffins say about diet and kids' behaviour and thinking. But be warned: some of the following flies in the face of established, hallowed and sacred wisdom.

The first holy grail to come tumbling down is the impact of sugar. There have been a zillion studies on the connections between sugar and hyperactivity, attention deficit disorder (ADD) and attention deficit hyperactivity disorder (ADHD). Overall, most of the good ones do not support the notion that sugar increases activity, impulsivity, locomotion or inattention, even in kids with established ADHD. In fact, some showed decreased activity levels after sugar intake and concluded that kids who are very active need more energy than sedentary peers and high sugar intakes actually help them cover their energy requirements.

So it's not so much that sugar makes them active, it's the opposite: the active kids need sugar! We're not saying load 'em up with 'empty calories' such as lollies and so on, but for kids who actually need the energy because they're very energetic, a bit of sugar here and there really doesn't hurt, especially if it makes otherwise nutritious food more palatable or they really enjoy it.

And not only do the studies fail to show too much in the way of adverse effects of sugar, they actually show an improvement in some aspects of intellectual performance following ingestion of a glucose load or some other carb-rich food. Studies have shown that glucose actually improves attention and reaction to frustration in children, as well as improving short-term memory, focused and sustained attention, maze learning, mathematical ability and a whole range of information-processing, recall and cognitive-processing tasks. These effects were shown not to be due to a correction of hypoglycaemia and have been reproduced across a whole range of baseline blood glucose levels.

In general, while not all mental tasks are improved following intake of sugar, the more demanding or the more effort required for the mental task, the more likely it is to be improved by glucose. But don't start filling your kids' lunch box with sweets. It rots their teeth.

Obviously it's not good to feed your kids pure glucose in a steady infusion to maximise their mental performance. On the other hand, it does show that the brain is sensitive to short-term fluctuations in glucose supply, so to get those sparks firing we need to maintain adequate levels of glycemia (blood sugar) between meals. One way to achieve this is by eating low glycemic index (GI) foods that slowly release glucose in the hours following ingestion, thereby maintaining sugar levels while minimising fluctuations between recess and lunch break. Some examples of good low GI carbs for kids include: baked beans, porridge, pasta/noodles, basmati or doongara rice, milk, fruit (apples, cherries, plums, grapes, strawberries, bananas, peaches, pears, oranges, mangoes), wholegrain bread, sweet potato, sushi, yoghurt, custard, low fat ice-cream, prunes, carrots, sweet corn and legumes.

[Frances Bellisle, 'Effects of diet on behaviour and cognition in children', *British Journal of Nutrition*, 92, suppl. 2, 2004, pp. 227–32.]

## 46. Is red cordial the devil?

You've spent their entire childhood associating monstrous behaviour with high sugar levels and artificial colouring additives. But while they always seem to return from birthday parties running in circles and screaming at the top of their lungs, it's not because of the red cordial.

Despite what we've been told, it seems artificial colours, preservatives and sweeteners don't make kids 'hyperactive'. While such additives in high doses may have detrimental effects on some kids who are already diagnosed as being hyperactive, even fairly massive levels exceeding what any child would consume from a regular diet have been shown to have no noticeable effect on the behaviour of normal, non-hyperactive kids. At moderate levels, even the most hyperactive kids were unaffected; it was only at very high doses that the hyperactive kids became more hyperactive. And there is no evidence to suggest that food additives cause children to become hyperactive in the first place.

[Frances Bellisle, 'Effects of diet on behaviour and cognition in children', *British Journal of Nutrition*, 92, suppl. 2, 2004, pp. 227–32.]

## 47. Breakfast and fish—was Grandma right?

How often have you been told that 'breakfast is the most important meal of the day' and missing breakfast will cause children to do poorly at school?

Extensive recent studies on the effects of having or missing breakfast have actually shown that it has variable effects—sometimes deleterious, sometimes beneficial and sometimes none at all—depending on whether the child is well-nourished in the first place, and what the task is, how long after breakfast it is performed, the child's IQ and age, whether or not the child is in the habit of regularly having or missing breakfast and the actual nutrient content and size of the breakfast consumed.

And when your grandmother told you fish was brain food, she wasn't kidding.

Thoughts go through the brain as electrical impulses, passing from one brain cell to the next through walls made out of fatty acids. Fish like salmon, mackerel and sardines have large amounts of a fatty acid called omega-3. Eating fish makes the walls of brain cells more elastic, so thoughts can pass through more easily. Scientists have found that eating fish once a week (or taking daily supplements) can improve reading, spelling and general behaviour.

*100 children between 5 and 12 years of age were given Omega 3 capsules with their food for 6 months. The daily dose of 6 capsules provided mega–3 fatty acids (558 mg of eicosapentaenoic acid and 174 mg of docosahexaenoic acid) and the Omega–6 fatty acid, linoleic acid (60 mg) plus 9.6 mg of vitamin E (natural form, alpha-tocopherol). 40 per cent showed clear improvement in reading, spelling, and behaviour. The capsules had an especially beneficial effect on children with ADHD.*

[A.J. Richardson & P. Montgomery, 'The Oxford–Durham Study: a randomized, controlled trial of dietary supplementation with fatty acids in children with developmental coordination disorder', *Pediatrics*, *115* (5), 2005, pp. 1360–66.]

## 48. How to make kids eat broccoli (and all the other healthy food they hate)

You beg them. Berate them. Bribe them. And at the end of dinner, the broccoli is either stuffed into a pot plant, hanging out of the dog's mouth or decorating the floor.

The interesting thing about food phobias is that kids' reluctance to try new foods (especially fruit and vegetables) is partly genetic, like blue eyes. So if you hate broccoli, or an older brother or sister hates broccoli, you are more likely to have a broccoli-hating baby.

The good news is that phobias are 100 per cent curable. Instead of promising to buy your kids a Nintendo Wii if they eat it, or to lock them in the basement if they don't, the best method is exposure. That means having broccoli on the table as much as possible. Don't make a big fuss whether they eat it or not. Eventually they will be hungry or forgetful enough to try a little bite—and discover that broccoli is not so bad after all. Frequent exposure increases the chances that a disliked food will eventually become liked.

[L.J. Cooke, C.M. Haworth & J. Wardle, 'Genetic and environmental influences on children's food neophobia', *The American Journal of Clinical Nutrition, 86* (2), 2007, pp. 428–33.]

## 49. The Tao of Bugs Bunny

There is a reason why Bugs Bunny is an enduring role model for children, and it's not just his chipper disposition and uncanny knack for outsmarting obnoxious bullies. Bugs loves his carrots, and all nutritionally conscious mothers should be pointing this out at every opportunity.

Carrots are orange because of a molecule called beta carotene. When you eat carrots, your body breaks down beta carotene into retinol, or vitamin A, which forms the pigment that absorbs light in your eyes. The first sign of a vitamin A deficiency is that you won't be able to see in dim lighting. A severe vitamin A deficiency can lead to blindness.

Lots of other foods have vitamin A, like eggs, milk, cereals, and most fruit and vegetables. But giving the biggest bang for your buck in terms of carotenoids are rockmelons, sweet potatoes, spinach and carrots.

As a guide, children should be eating a carrot a day (100 g which has about 835 micrograms of carotene—kids need between 500 and 900 micrograms a day). It's true that you can turn orange from eating too many carrots, but this condition (called carotonemia—eating too many carotenoids), although a little startling, is entirely harmless and goes away once you decrease your carotene intake.

So whether it's wabbit season or duck season, make sure there are carrots on the side.

[G. Giuliano, S. Al-Babili & J. von Lintig, 'Carotenoid oxygenases: cleave it or leave it', *Trends in Plant Science, 8* (4), 2003, pp. 145–9.]

## 50. Can vitamins make your kids smarter?

Traditionally, kids took vitamins to keep them healthy. But now it looks like vitamins can make kids smarter too.

Vitamins are chemicals that your body can't make by itself. Until the twentieth century, humans relied on eating and drinking to give us all the vitamins we needed, and cultures all over the world recognised the benefits of certain foods. The ancient Egyptians knew eating liver could cure night blindness, which is caused by a deficiency in vitamin A. Captain Cook prevented scurvy in his crew by feeding them spinach, which is high in vitamin C.

Now we can take concentrated vitamins in the form of pills, capsules, and powdered drinks. The crucial vitamins are A, B (1, 2, 3, 5, 6 and 12), C, D, E, folate, iron, zinc, chromium, manganese, molybdenum, selenium and copper. If that sounds too much like a periodic table to remember, a good multivitamin has most of the vitamins your body needs.

The importance for children is that, amongst other things, vitamins help our brains to function properly. In fact, children who have low levels of vitamins in their blood can show abnormal brain activity. In contrast, children who have sufficient vitamin levels score 2.5 to 15 IQ points higher than children who don't.

Of course, you can get the same effect with a well-balanced diet. But just to be sure, multivitamins have got it covered.

Thiamine deficiency is a problem for kids, usually

teens, who have a truly unbalanced, nutritionally bereft 'junk food' diet. It can lead to irritability, aggressive behaviour and personality changes. A study of irritable, aggressive kids with very nutritionally poor diets found that while they failed to respond to medication or psychotherapy, their behaviour improved as a result of thiamine supplementation alone. Supplements are only beneficial if your kid is actually thiamine deficient in the first place, though, hyper-dosing them won't do anything much as the body stores of thiamine are relatively small and can be depleted within a few weeks of inadequate intake. So they need to eat a normal, nutritious diet on an ongoing basis. Boring but true.

[S.J. Schoenthaler et al., 'The effect of vitamin-mineral supplementation on the intelligence of American schoolchildren: a randomised, double-blind placebo-controlled trial', *The Journal of Alternative and Complementary Medicine*, 6 (1), 2000, pp. 19–29.]

## 51. Make reading time fun

Bedtime stories are an essential part of childhood, but what do they mean to you, as a parent? Is it a fun bonding experience for you and your child, or do you pick the shortest stories you can find then rush through them so you can turn off the lights and get back to your favourite TV show?

There is no doubt that reading stories to your kids daily improves their reading comprehension, but it's also *how* you read them that counts. Children with parents who are engaged with the stories, use a variety of voices, and take the time to answer questions and explain the story are more motivated to read later on. This means not only will they have higher reading skills, but they will probably develop a love of reading that will carry on into their lives.

There are millions of children's books out there, and local libraries offer an extensive—and free—selection. Find ones that don't bore you, with characters you find interesting—perhaps stories you remember enjoying when you were a child. Make story time a fun time for both of you.

[S. Sonnenschein & K. Munsterman, 'The influence of home-based reading interactions on 5-year-olds' reading motivations and early literacy development', *Early Childhood Research Quarterly*, *17* (3), 2000, pp. 318–37.]

## 52. Where do I come from?

It's the question every parent hears sooner or later. But how correct should your answer be? If it pops up just after your toddler starts walking, should you give them penises and vaginas straight up, or should you feed them a Dr Seuss birds and bees poem that doesn't really make any sense?

If you do go with a 'delivered by the stork' angle, at what age should you tell them you were lying and *then* hit them with the penises and vaginas story?

The good news is that kids already have a vague idea about procreation. Even at the age of five, they know that puppies come from dogs and kittens come from cats, so it's not such a stretch to conclude babies come from people.

How much of this process you explain is really up to you. You can always start off with the fact that babies come from inside mummy's tummy, and build on it as you think appropriate.

*Four- to seven-year-olds were told stories where a baby was born to an animal of one species (for example, a horse) but was adopted and raised by an animal of another species (for example, a cow). When asked to explicitly predict the species of the baby, even five-year-olds were able to reliably judge that the baby would be of the same species as the birth parent rather than the adoptive parent. This result suggests that even at five years old, children have some understanding about the biological cause of birth.*

[S.C. Johnson & G.E.A. Solomon, 'Why dogs have puppies and cats have kittens: the role of birth in young children's understanding of biological origins', *Child Development*, 68 (3), 1997, pp. 404–19.]

## 53. Take the time to show them

You may have heard of discovery learning, which is based on the theory that children who make discoveries on their own retain information longer and are better able to build on that information. The reasoning behind discovery learning is that it doesn't matter how many times people tell you something, you have to figure it out for yourself for it to really make sense.

But new research has revealed that children actually learn *better* when someone takes the time to explain things or show them what to do. Which makes sense: how long does it take you to figure out a new gadget if no one shows you how to use it? Sure, you might get more satisfaction figuring out how to GPS-track your spouse on your iPhone by yourself, but how much time did you waste figuring it out on your own? The extraordinary ability of children to imitate and build on information is one of the unique qualities that makes us human.

So work with that. Whether it's riding a bike, or telling the story of how the earth was formed, take the time to demonstrate or explain how it all works. Encourage their curiosity, and if you don't know the answer, do the research together. They will learn and understand more than if they did it alone and will build on it in the future.

[D. Klahr & M. Nigam, 'The equivalence of learning paths in early science instruction', *Psychological Science*, 15 (10), 2004, pp. 661–7.]

## 54. School before school

In the race to help our children get ahead, there has been an explosion of preschool programs that promise to make your kids smarter before they hit school. After four years, you hand them a backpack with lunch and pencil case and push them out the door, satisfied that learning is out of your hands and they are now someone else's problem.

But what are you really getting for your money? A study of US kindergartens showed that preschool definitely raises maths and reading levels, but that this effect tends to disappear by first grade. And these results can come at a price—you might notice your kids bringing home an attitude problem as some studies suggest that kids who attend preschool show an increase in aggressive behaviour. They might fight or argue more, get angry more frequently, and have reduced self-control, where they are disrespectful of other people's property and can't seem to harness their temper.

According to this study, the only time preschool seems to benefit kids is when they come from a lower socio-economic background. But for the rest of them, if you're going to enrol them, you might see an improvement in results but you may have to work harder at keeping them in line.

[K.A. Magnuson & J. Waldfogel, 'Does prekindergarten improve school preparation and performance?', *Economics of Education Review*, *26* (1), 2007, pp. 33–51.]

## 55. Mind reading

We depend on our ability to read other people's minds. Does my boss know I'm surfing the net right now? Does my husband think I look fat in this dress? Is she really my friend or is she just pretending?

As you can imagine, our ability to read other people's thoughts, or at least guess them, is a very useful skill. Children develop this ability, called 'theory of mind', between three and five years of age, and the earlier the better.

Children who develop theory of mind at an early age tend to have more friends and be more social. Children who develop it later are often less social and are sometimes bullied. This can make school difficult, as it's harder to make friends once friendship groups have already formed.

You can help your children's mind-reading abilities by talking to them about what other people are thinking and feeling. 'Do you think Daddy knows we're home?' or 'Do you think Katie would like this dress?' are questions that start kids thinking about the thoughts of others, and will kickstart their theory of mind development.

[C. Peterson & V. Slaughter, 'Opening windows into the mind: mothers' preferences for mental state explanations and children's theory of mind', *Cognitive Development, 18* (3), 2003, pp. 399–429.]

## 56. Does Mozart make you smarter?

There was a craze a while back where some parents played Mozart to their kids to make them smarter. The idea started after scientists claimed that listening to Mozart improved spatial skills, which help people figure out maps and interpret technical drawings.

Researchers went nuts, trying to figure out whether the improvement was limited to Mozart or could be replicated in music from Beethoven to the Red Hot Chili Peppers.

It was a nice thought. Unfortunately, most of the subsequent studies found that the Mozart effect wasn't all it was cracked up to be. Even studies that supported the Mozart effect found the improvement in spatial skills only lasted around fifteen minutes. The positive result could be because the upbeat notes of Mozart give us an enlivening emotional sensation, and when we feel better, we tend to remember more.

However, there is evidence that *learning* music can improve IQ. Researchers think this is because music lessons develop a range of abilities, such as focusing on a task, daily practice, memorising, refining fine motor skills, and transferring emotion into the performance. It seems these skills are important during the childhood years when kids' brains are highly plastic and extremely sensitive to their environment.

So if you believe it, ditch the Mozart and buy the kids some music lessons.

[E.G. Schellenberg, 'Music lessons enhance IQ', *Psychological Science*, 15 (8), 2004, pp. 511–514. L. Waterhouse, 'Multiple intelligences, the Mozart effect, and emotional intelligence: a critical review', *Educational Psychologist*, 41 (4), 2006, pp. 207–25.]

## 57. Ready and eager to learn

'What colour's the balloon?' asks Adam of a small group of kids, including his three-year-old daughter, Ellie. 'Blue,' shoots back five-year-old Anton with a hint of disdain.

Adults try to teach kids in lots of formal or informal ways by demonstrating, informing, explaining or questioning, Socratic style. Kids don't always realise when this is happening, especially if no learning occurs—either because the child doesn't understand the lesson or, as in Anton's case, because they already know the answer. According to one definition, teaching is 'an intentional activity to increase the knowledge or understanding of another'. In other words, regardless of the outcome (full, partial or no learning), teaching can be said to have taken place as long as an effort to teach has been made.

In order to teach another person, the teacher needs to recognise a lack of knowledge in others. And in turn, the potential student needs to realise the intention behind the lesson. Anton realised that *he* knew the balloon's colour and would have expected that a big grown-up like Adam would know too. What Anton did not take account of was that Ellie and the other younger kids might be still learning their colours, and that Adam was trying to teach them.

Kids must often wonder why people, especially adults, ask such silly questions. As they get older it becomes less of a mystery. Indeed, knowing that someone is trying to teach them something may well make them concentrate more, even if the questions themselves seem somewhat naff.

The fact that most kids become more insightful at about age five is just one of the reasons starting school around this age makes sense. School readiness is more than merely cognitive ability and specific skills in literacy, numeracy and social understanding. If kids also have some understanding that school is about teaching and learning, school will seem less 'boring' or 'pointless' and the kids will be more able to take an active role in what's going on around them.

[Margalit Ziv et al., 'Young children's recognition of the intentionality of teaching', *Child Development*, vol. 79, no. 5, Sept/Oct 2008, pp. 1237–56.]

## 58. Single-sex versus co-ed schools

The debate over whether single-sex or co-educational schools provide superior educational, socio-emotional or other developmental benefits to boys, girls or society at large is one that will probably never end. Ultimately, though, being able to tailor one's choice to the child is the most important thing. And be aware that what works for one child will not necessarily be best for his or her siblings, so be willing to balance all the pros and cons for each individual as well as for the family.

The arguments for and against single-sex versus co-ed schooling are numerous and highly contentious. And while most of these arguments have their merits, many of us will have a gut feeling about what is best for our kids, often based on our personal experiences as well as those of friends, family, contemporaries and elders. And there's also the issue of what's actually available to us in terms of affordability, access and agreement.

And it is here that the research findings (particularly those in favour of single-sex schooling) become really interesting, since the *selection bias* created by the nature and background of the people making the choices (or even by the luxury of having a choice) is significant.

The fact is that single-sex schools are usually private or selective schools, often drawing their students from families of higher socioeconomic status or educational background. Separating out the benefits attributable to the type of school (single-sex or co-ed) versus the benefits attributable to differences in student body and family background, attitudes and educational environment is the real challenge. Plus, single-sex schools usually have more applicants than places which creates a competitive market, so it's the families with the requisite financial, cultural and social resources, who know how the game is played (and won), who usually gain entry.

According to some studies, once background and ability are adequately controlled for, there is no real evidence of academic superiority either for single-sex or co-ed schools.

Factors such as school size, student–teacher ratios, religious philosophies, religious homogeneity and socio-economic status of students at single-sex and co-ed schools are obviously important confounding factors outside of the issue of whether girls and boys are separated or not. Interestingly, the prevalence of sexism amongst staff and students was not necessarily related to whether the student body was single-sex or mixed; the challenge of advancing social equity and gender understanding was the same for both types of schools.

In the end, our decisions and our children's preferences will be guided by a number of different and possibly competing factors: from perceived educational and socio-emotional benefits to the 'old school tie' and parents' ideas about social status, to the child's wish to remain with his or her buddies, to more rarefied academic or theoretical arguments.

Ultimately, however logically or illogically, it can come down to our own experience. If we attended a single-sex school and loved it we will be swayed that way, and vice versa. But perhaps what's really important is making a decision that the whole family can live with, and that will foster a happy, emotionally resilient child.

[Richard Harker, 'Achievement, gender and the single-sex/co-ed debate', *British Journal of Sociology of Education*, vol. 21, no. 2, 2000, pp. 203–18. Fred A. Mael, 'Single-sex and coeducational schooling: Relationships to socio-emotional and academic development', *Review of Educational Research*, Summer 1998; vol. 68, no. 2, pp. 101–29.]

## 59. Is the teacher a good witch or a bad witch?

Before you enrol your child in a school, ask if you can meet their kindergarten teacher. If the teacher is a warm person who loves the job and cares about kids, then your child has a better chance of having a positive interaction. If the teacher reminds you of the witch from Hansel and Gretel and seems more likely to cook your child in an oven than provide a nurturing environment, find another class or another school.

After you, the kindergarten teacher is the most important adult in your child's life. The teacher will spend as much time with your child as you and stand as an authority figure, moral compass and source of information. The kind of relationship your child has with the kindergarten teacher will predict behaviour and academic performance as far as year 8.

Go to parent–teacher nights. Gauge how the teacher talks and feels about your child. If the report is 'doing well but could try harder', there may be little cause for alarm. But if you get a vibe that the teacher would be happy never to see your child again, it's time to take action.

And if your five-year-old ever comes home and says, 'My teacher hates me,' take it seriously and find a solution.

*Kindergarten teachers' reports of negativity in relation to students uniquely predicted student grades, standardized test scores and work habits through lower elementary [primary] school. It also predicted behavioural outcomes into upper elementary and middle schools.*

[B.K. Hamre & R.C. Pianta, 'Early teacher–child relationships and the trajectory of children's school outcomes through eighth grade', *Child Development*, 72 (2), 2001, pp. 625–38.]

## 60. IQ: Nature or nurture?

In the past, research has suggested that IQ is more dependent on your genetic makeup than your environment. However, within educationally impoverished families, environmental influences might play a greater role than previously thought.

A recent study found that amongst kids with more highly educated parents, environmental effects had no significant impact on their IQ at all. But when it came to kids with less well educated parents (high school only or less), the effect of shared environmental factors was much greater and genetic inheritance played a smaller role.

One explanation is that in families with highly educated parents the environment is generally average or above average in terms of opportunities for educational enrichment and intellectual stimulation, so variation in IQ as a result of environmental differences is fairly flat. On the other hand, in less educated, less stimulating, less privileged family environments, IQ may be more sensitive to such environmental differences. Generally speaking, kids from the least educated families generally have the lowest IQs and kids from the most highly educated families have the highest IQs. But studies have found that children born into poor families who are adopted by affluent families often make significant IQ gains in their new environment.

Interestingly, in educated families, IQ is still largely determined by inherited factors regardless of the quality of the home environment. Perhaps this is because bright kids can extract information from their environments more rapidly, handle complex information better and expose themselves to information at a greater rate than less able kids can. In addition, brighter kids are more able to make up for—or improve on—the quality of their home environment through stimulation from school and peer groups. Kids from less educated families, in addition to being possibly less genetically endowed IQ-wise, may also be less able to find the intellectual stimulation they need in less well educated communities.

If you are a highly educated parent with bright young kids, encouraging your child's interest and engagement with the world and facilitating this will help them reach their full intellectual potential.

If, however, you're less well educated, you can help your kids achieve their best by making education and intellectual pursuits a priority, and by valuing activities that involve thinking, reasoning, analysis, discussion, logical debate and questioning. You can also help your child find extra educational resources and other opportunities to stimulate and challenge their mind.

[David C. Rowe et al., 'Genetic and environmental influences on vocabulary IQ: Parental education level as moderator', *Child Development*, *70* (5), Sept/Oct 1999, pp. 1151–62.]

## 61. Teach your kids to have a winning attitude

Many of us will have heard the story of the *Little Engine That Could*. The red train that had a bummer of a hill to climb. By chanting 'I think I can' over and over, the train made it to its destination.

Kids face a life full of challenges. Something as simple as tying shoelaces can be a bewildering mass of knots and loops. But while it might be tempting, easier and quicker to tie the shoelaces for them, it is important to let kids do things for themselves, to encourage them as much as possible, and to give them faith in themselves.

When faced with a challenge, there are two options. The helpless model is when someone gives up, assumes they don't have what it takes to tie the shoelace, will never be able to tie the shoelace, and maybe even experiences panic and fear at the thought of tying the shoelace.

Then there is the mastery model. They persist with the shoelace. If they can't do it, they assume it's because they aren't trying hard enough and need more time. And if they still can't do it, they are sure they will crack it next time.

It's important to teach your kids the mastery approach or, as some call it, a winning attitude.

Kids who have a winning attitude early, around age five or six, will carry this attitude through primary school. Conquering the shoelaces will lead to conquering calculus later on in life.

[D.I. Ziegert et al., 'Longitudinal study of young children's responses to challenging achievement situations', *Child Development*, 72 (2), 2001, pp. 609–24.]

## 62. Personal bests

When pursuing educational goals, do you or your child tend to value learning as an end in itself, focusing on mastering the task at hand and enjoying the intrinsic rewards of doing so? Or are you more focused on goals external to the task, such as winning prizes, coming first and beating others, or gaining social or parental approval?

Students tend to fall into one of the following two categories: those who compare their current performance with their previous achievements, and those who compare their performance with the achievements of their classmates or peers.

When students set challenging goals for themselves that are specific and easily measured in the short term, they gain a better sense of their own progress. Such self-satisfaction from improving their own performance in turn enhances their sense of personal achievement. This makes them inclined to set ever more challenging goals for themselves, creating more motivation to revise learning strategies to meet these new personal goals.

Regardless of whether goals are set or not, children who are more focused on their own progress show significantly higher skill and enhanced sense of personal achievement than kids who compare themselves with others. Kids who fall into the latter category may become less willing to perform tasks and set progressively lower goals over time.

Self-comparison, rather than comparison with peers or competitors, leads to improved performance and an increased motivation to learn. Students who concentrate on self-improvement, rather than focusing on competing with others, tend to engage more actively in learning tasks and become more skilled and efficient at them. By contrast, kids who are preoccupied with their performance and ability relative to others have higher anxiety levels, which interferes with their engagement with the task and as a result hinders their ability. In particular, comparing oneself against students with superior ability or scores tends to heighten self-doubt.

As parents, it is natural to want to know how your child is performing relative to his or her peers, but an excessive preoccupation with this can have negative consequences, particularly if it invites repeatedly negative comparisons.

Aiming for higher marks, more prizes or a higher ranking in the class is potentially fraught with stress and anxiety. Being dux, winning all the awards and getting into the most highly desired university course may be profoundly satisfying for the rare individual who achieves it, however it is simply not going to happen for the majority of students. Comparing oneself with the academic stars of the year (or cousins, parents, oft-lauded family friends, acquaintances or 'local legends') can be a real downer as well as totally counter-productive. This sort of comparison might see your child start to set lower and lower goals, using the excuse that they never really tried or wanted to succeed rather than taking personal responsibility and applying themselves.

You can't always be the best at something but you can always aim for a 'personal best'. These are the goals we should encourage our kids to set for themselves.

[Shu-Shen Shih & Joyce M. Alexander, 'Interacting effects of goal setting and self- or other-referenced feedback on children's development of self-efficacy and cognitive skill within the Taiwanese classroom', *Journal of Educational Psychology*, *92* (3), 2000, pp. 536–43.]

## 63. Spell it out

There's a lot of focus on kids learning to read, but less on learning to spell—which is equally important. In fact, how well kids can spell and recognise the sounds letters make at an early age predicts how well they will be able to read later on in school.

You can help by sounding out words while you read to them—not naming the letters, but sounding them out. So 'a' can be a short 'a' as in 'cat' or a long 'a' as in 'cake'. Sounding out the different parts of words as you read them helps with spelling (for example, 'ko-a-la').

So pause a little over story time to sound words out phonologically (fo-no-loj-i-cal-lee) and your kids will be spelling and reading better in no time.

[M. Caravolas, C. Hulme & M.J. Snowling, 'The foundations of spelling ability: evidence from a 3-year longitudinal study', *Journal of Memory and Language*, 45 (4), 2001, pp. 751–74.]

## 64. Talk like a scientist

Throughout their school years, children need to be able to think like a scientist. Besides memorising, they will have to learn to challenge ideas, suggest hypotheses, and choose between conflicting explanations.

The most helpful thing you can do in this regard is to show your kids how to *talk* like a scientist. It's easy for different thoughts and ideas to get muddled, and one of the most useful skills is to talk it through. So, for instance, when talking about a subject like botany, instead of giving a big monologue about everything *you* know, get your kids to talk about what *they* know, like how trees grow, why trees need water and soil, the role of leaves and flowers. Help talk them through problems logically, ask them lots of questions, and get them to think about what they are saying and whether it makes sense.

Teaching you children to use language as a reasoning tool will help clarify their thinking and improve their performance right through school, especially in maths and science.

[N. Mercer et al., 'Reasoning as a scientist: ways of helping children to use language to learn science', *British Educational Research Journal*, 30 (3), 2004, pp. 359–77.]

## 65. The building blocks of maths

If children find themselves struggling with maths early on, they can end up feeling like they're behind the eight ball forever. Getting your children off to a positive start with maths is important.

A certain amount of maths ability is innate, and it all starts with counting. From about the age of four months, babies can discriminate one object from two and two objects from three. And by five months babies can understand the consequences of adding or subtracting small numbers of objects from a larger group of objects. By age three or four, children can discriminate between as many as four to six objects and they can almost instantly recognise how many objects are present in a row of one to four, only needing to count to be sure when there are five or more.

By age three to four, kids generally understand the five counting principles implicitly:

1. They should assign one and only one number word to each object (one-one principle).
2. They should always assign the numbers in the same order (stable order principle).
3. The last count indicates the number of objects in the set (cardinal principle).
4. The order in which objects are counted is irrelevant (order irrelevance principle).
5. These principles apply to any set of objects (abstraction principle).

They may make a few mistakes, missing a number or counting something twice, but their intention is usually clear. Even when they skip or misorder certain digits—1, 2, 3, 4, 6, 8, 9—they tend to do so consistently, showing that they at least understand the stable order of numbers.

It's worth encouraging and practising counting from early on—initially simply as a series of words that run together, then later by helping your child grasp how the number words relate to a quantity and showing them how this can be found by counting objects or pictures of objects on a page.

Your child has natural mathematical ability right from the age of four months. Harness that ability and use it in your everyday conversations and interactions. How many biscuits? How many grapes? How many arms on Henry the Octopus? How many spots on the dog? How many minutes until *Play School* starts? How many presents did you get? How old are you? How many days until Christmas? How many times have I asked you . . .? There is no end to the number of ways you can make maths relevant, useful and alive for your child, and the rewards will add and multiply.

[Robert S. Siegler, 'Implications of cognitive science research for mathematics education' in J. Kilpatrick et al. (eds), *A Research Companion to Principles and Standards for School Mathematics*, National Council of Teachers of Mathematics, Reston, VA, 2003, pp. 219–33.]

# 66. Overcoming stumbling blocks with maths

International studies have shown that kids in East Asia perform markedly better than kids in the West on standardised maths tests. While this discrepancy is often blamed on inferior formal instruction in the West, in fact substantial differences in maths knowledge exist between East Asian and Western kids even before they have received formal maths lessons, suggesting that the differences in achievement in fact reflect cultural differences in the way maths is learned.

Once kids start school, they need to absorb and apply mathematical concepts and principles as well as procedures and facts. If they fail to grasp and connect the concepts and principles that underlie the procedures, they may well generate flawed procedures and systematic patterns of errors. Recognising such patterns of errors and being able to pinpoint the underlying misunderstanding provides an opportunity for teachers and parents to specifically correct them. And recognising the 'bugs' or incorrect application of rules that a child is habitually making (for example, in multi-digit subtraction, interpreting 0 − 8 as being the same as 8 − 0) allows you to deal with that particular area of misunderstanding.

Research shows that while such 'bugs' are common amongst American kids, they are far less common amongst Korean kids. The reason for this seems to be that Korean kids have a firmer grasp of the base-10 system and its relation to 'borrowing' in multi-digit subtraction. This understanding of the fact that the position of a digit in a number reflects whether it represents units, tens, hundreds and so on is crucial to a lot of maths.

Learning to read numbers and understand what a line of digits in a row actually represents requires understanding of the meaning and significance of each digit's position within the number. Teaching kids this and making sure they actually understand it deeply enough to be able to apply it is vital. You can't assume a child understands a concept just because it has been explained once or twice and seems obvious to most of us. If your child doesn't understand, it doesn't necessarily mean they 'can't do maths'. If you or someone else can commit to specifically showing them, if necessary over and over again, perhaps they can.

Looking for and finding 'bugs' in kids' maths understanding or execution is vital for 'debugging' them. If they can be consistent in committing errors which reveal the presence of 'bugs', why not 'debug' them so they can be equally consistent in executing correct procedures? In getting the right answers they also receive all the rewards that brings: satisfaction, confidence, pleasure and joy of discovery, and a well-earned sense of achievement.

[Robert S. Siegler, 'Implications of cognitive science research for mathematics education' in J. Kilpatrick et al. (eds), *A Research Companion to Principles and Standards for School Mathematics*, National Council of Teachers of Mathematics, Reston, VA, 2003, pp. 219–33.]

## 67. Maths strategies

Finding fractions difficult is not limited to primary or secondary school students. Even some adults in community college maths classes think $\frac{1}{2} + \frac{1}{3} = \frac{2}{5}$. And there are lots of kids who think 2.357 is bigger than 2.86 because 357 is bigger than 86, or that 2.43 is larger than 2.897 because .897 involves thousandths whereas .43 involves hundredths, and hundredths are always going to be bigger than thousandths.

Certain basic misunderstandings about the meanings of different number representations, or a failure to link understanding with specific procedures, leads to these systematic, recurrent and persistent errors. Algebra is another area where kids can become confused and start believing they're incapable of doing maths.

In order to avoid these problems, it is vital that your child and teacher work together to isolate the specific concepts and procedures that the child is trying to master. The teacher needs to provide instruction, examples and practice exercises so that the child can learn the necessary skills and gain a true understanding. Then they'll have a basis from which to anticipate the common traps and tricks that arise.

In maths, as in many other areas of learning, there are often several different ways of solving any particular problem. Some of these strategies are more advanced and sophisticated, and usually quicker and more accurate, whereas others rely on more basic skills such as counting on your fingers.

Although past research has suggested that children have a 'staircase' approach to learning, whereby they progressively move upwards using more and more advanced approaches over time, some recent studies have found that kids continue to use a variety of strategies, both less and more advanced, from early childhood to adolescence and beyond.

This tendency to use a variety of approaches is a spontaneous feature of kids' thinking and usually defies intervention by teachers. For example, many teachers will discourage or even attempt to forbid kids from working out sums by adding on their fingers, but this rarely works; kids will simply hide their fingers and continue with this strategy until they develop sufficient knowledge and proficiency using other methods. Furthermore, forbidding kids from using their preferred method without strengthening their understanding and proficiency in more advanced procedures may result in them making more errors.

Kids who use a variety of different strategies for solving problems tend to learn better, perhaps in part because this approach lends itself to solving a wider range of problems. Understanding why certain different strategies will result in the same answer while other superficially similar (but in fact not equivalent) strategies result in different answers helps to build deeper understanding.

Some studies have found that when deciding on the appropriate problem-solving strategy, kids from different socioeconomic backgrounds are equally capable of being systematic and sensitive to the characteristics of the problem. However, kids from lower-income backgrounds often don't do as well because of poorer execution of strategies and less practice at solving problems. It is not necessarily a matter of being less capable of higher-level thought but one of gaining adequate practice and good instruction.

Any child can do maths, some kids may just need more help. Finding a tutor or seeking out additional advice and exercises from your child's teacher are both worth considering. Practice makes perfect, or at least proficient. So even if you had difficulties with basic maths it doesn't mean your child will, if you help them, get some help or both.

[Robert S. Siegler, 'Implications of cognitive science research for mathematics education' in J. Kilpatrick et al. (eds), *A Research Companion to Principles and Standards for School Mathematics*, National Council of Teachers of Mathematics, Reston, VA, 2003, pp. 219–33.]

## 68. Making maths easier—for everyone

When it comes to mathematical ability, kids fall into three broad groups: not-so-good students, good students and perfectionists. Compared to the not-so-good ones, the good students are faster, more accurate, use more advanced strategies and perform better in standardised maths achievement tests.

Perfectionists are just as accurate as the good students and have equally high scores for maths and IQ but may choose a higher proportion of slow and effortful strategies to solve problems. These kids prefer not to rely on memory unless they are totally sure, if necessary reverting to counting up from one to check. And whereas good students will have more confidence in their ability to recall answers without checking, perfectionists like to make doubly sure.

In an exam situation, if your child tends towards a perfectionist approach it is worth encouraging them to choose the quickest method for solving a maths problem in the first instance, then checking the answer using alternative methods later only if time permits.

In a recent study, roughly half of the kids in the not-so-good category ended up being classified as having a mathematical disability, an assessment that takes into account poor class performance as well as poor test scores. These kids have difficulty recalling answers or figuring them out using basic strategies, and they tend to use immature counting procedures and execute them slowly and inaccurately. As they progress through school, these kids encounter further problems when trying to master more advanced maths which requires them to build on basic mathematical foundations that may still, for them, be somewhat shaky.

Learning maths requires having sufficient 'working memory' to hold the original problem in your head long enough to compute the answer, so the question and the answer can be associated. Mathematically disabled kids tend to have poorer working memory and therefore less capacity to hold numerical information in their heads compared to their same-age peers. They also tend to have a poorer conceptual understanding of maths operations and counting, adding yet further obstacles to their maths learning.

To overcome difficulties or at least improve proficiency in maths, three issues need to be recognised and addressed: poor backgound knowledge, poor processing capacity, and poor conceptual understanding.

If your child is struggling with maths, it's important to help them understand the most crucial concepts of maths—assuming you understand them yourself sufficiently to explain them. If you don't, it may be worth engaging a tutor who is reasonably patient, encouraging and sensitive to assist them.

There's a lot more to maths and maths instruction than just sitting down and doing it. Kids who are more naturally talented at grasping concepts quickly and applying procedures swiftly and accurately tend to enjoy maths and engage in it willingly and purposefully. However, everyone is capable of doing maths to a certain level. Kids who lag behind with maths need tailored instruction to pinpoint and remedy areas of poor understanding as well as extra practice to improve accuracy, speed, recall and confidence. Once they develop a deeper understanding, they are more likely to engage purposefully. And once they engage purposefully, they are more likely to think analytically and develop even deeper understandings.

[Robert S. Siegler, 'Implications of cognitive science research for mathematics education' in J. Kilpatrick et al. (eds), *A Research Companion to Principles and Standards for School Mathematics*, National Council of Teachers of Mathematics, Reston, VA, 2003, pp. 219–33.]

## 69. Encouraging curiosity

One of the central reasons for maths education is that it encourages analytic thinking. Analysis requires that we distinguish features that cause certain events from features that simply accompany them. Knowing which maths technique is necessary for solving a particular problem requires analysis of why that technique works or doesn't work. This is a skill everyone needs.

Kids who try to deeply understand a topic, concept or process become more engaged in learning it than kids who just accept what they are told without thinking. Likewise, when kids have a reason or purpose for wanting to learn about or understand something, they are more inclined to analyse it to do so. And kids who actively engage in understanding how and why things work are also more likely to transfer what they learn to new situations and contexts.

One way of encouraging analytic thinking in kids is to ask them to explain how they arrived at a correct answer or conclusion. This requires kids to generate the underlying logic for themselves. And encouraging kids to explain other people's reasoning in a variety of contexts can eventually lead to them reflexively asking similar questions of themselves. They can then become automatically, purposefully engaged in a wide variety of situations where they'll practise transferring and applying knowledge to different problems.

Asking kids why certain answers are incorrect also encourages analytic thinking and reasoning. In Japanese classrooms, where excellent levels of maths achievement occur, kids are frequently asked to explain why an answer is right or wrong. An American study that replicated this approach found increased learning amongst kids who were asked to explain why answers were both right *and* wrong, as opposed to just asking why answers were correct or just asking for the answers.

So whether it's maths or any other topic, it's worth taking the time to consider 'why' and 'why not'. The more you think, the better you get at it, the more questions you ask, the more answers you generate, and that generates yet further questions and answers. Feed kids' curiosity about not just what is and what isn't but also *why* and *why not*. Encourage them to ask questions and generate answers; give them feedback but also give them the opportunity to tell you why they might be right or wrong.

This Socratic style of teaching—where kids learn through questioning and debating, by analysing arguments for and against various conclusions—deepens their understanding and, more importantly, increases their powers of reasoning and the depth of their engagement with the world. It adds up really.

[Robert S. Siegler, 'Implications of cognitive science research for mathematics education' in J. Kilpatrick et al. (eds), *A Research Companion to Principles and Standards for School Mathematics*, National Council of Teachers of Mathematics, Reston, VA, 2003, pp. 219–33.]

## 70. How to help them with their homework

You want them to do well at school, but how far should you go? You wouldn't be the first parent to touch up a school assignment in Photoshop, or finish off maths homework in Excel, but how will your child learn? And if your child is struggling with their homework, when should you step in, and when should you let them figure it out for themselves?

There is no formula for how much of your child's homework you are allowed to contribute to. The best approach is based on common sense and good judgment. You have to help them in a way where they eventually succeed at the task *and* learn the skills they need to complete the task on their own next time. So work out how much they understand, then give them enough information so they can figure it out for themselves. Give them specific instructions when they are stuck, then leave them alone when you can see they are getting somewhere. This ensures your child has some success as well as making them feel they had some part in that success, giving them the confidence to go it alone next time.

> *Parents' scaffolding behaviour was significantly associated with academic competence in the longer term, as shown by the links between scaffolding behaviour and teacher- and child-report of academic abilities. These findings suggest that the beneficial effects of scaffolding may extend to the achievement of broader academic goals desired by teachers and parents. It is possible that parents who routinely teach their children tasks by building on what their children already know, boost their children's*

*self-esteem regarding academic tasks and, in turn, help their*
*children remain motivated at school.*

[J.F. Mattanah et al., 'Authoritative parenting, parental scaffolding of long-division mathematics, and children's academic competence in fourth grade', *Journal of Applied Developmental Psychology*, 26 (1), 2005, pp. 85–106.]

## 71. Overcoming reading problems

Tom Cruise, Sir Richard Branson, Orlando Bloom, Keira Knightley, Jaime Oliver, Keanu Reeves, Walt Disney, Harrison Ford, Robin Williams, Winston Churchill, Thomas Edison, Alexander Graham Bell, Hans Christian Anderson, Gustave Flaubert, John Lennon, Andy Warhol and even Albert Einstein are just some of the luminaries who are widely known or believed to have (or have had) dyslexia. Reading disability, known as 'developmental dyslexia', is one of the most common neurobehavioural problems of children and adults. And while Cruise, Disney and Einstein et al. have shown it's not necessarily a barrier to an illustrious career, dyslexia can be difficult to live with, especially when you're at school.

Reading difficulty can seriously affect a child's academic progress, confidence and self-esteem. Many kids with a reading disability end up believing they are stupid or slow and grow to hate school. While there are a variety of reading interventions on offer to assist struggling readers, it's hard to know what is going to work best.

The central problem in reading disability is to do with phonology—basically the ability to understand and interpret the underlying sound structure of words, or phonemes. (Phonemes are the units of sound, represented by letters or combinations of letters, that make up each word and distinguish each word from another e.g. p, b, d, t as in pad, pat, bad, bat.) With this in mind, a recent study looked at the impact of interventions targeting phonology in kids aged six to nine to see if this led to more 'fluent' reading.

In addition to assessing their reading fluency before and after eight months of reading intervention, the researchers used magnetic resonance imaging (MRI) to measure the children's brain activity while they performed phonological letter-identification tasks to see if actual visible changes were occurring.

Not only did the children who received the phonologically based reading intervention make significantly greater gains in reading ability and fluency (compared with kids who got standard 'special ed' or 'remedial reading' interventions), they also had greatly increased activity patterns in the left hemisphere of their brains, similar to those of good readers. Follow-up MRIs one year after the intervention ended showed that these kids were still activating more sites of the brain associated with language and reading than they had before the intervention.

So what exactly was this phonologically based intervention?

The intervention was conducted by certified teachers who had undergone an extensive training program, and it consisted of fifty minutes of daily individual tutoring focused on helping the kids grasp the principles of how letters and letter combinations represent different phonemes. Each lesson was built around the following five components:

1. reviewing sound-symbol associations;
2. practising phoneme analysis and blending, by moving Scrabble tiles around to make new words;
3. timed reading of learned words to develop fluency;

4. reading stories out loud; and
5. dictation of words with phonetically regular spelling sound patterns (for example, dog or cat rather than 'onomatopoiea' or 'psychiatry').

Reading is not only important for kids to help make their way in the world, it can also be a source of profound pleasure and delight, inspiration and instruction. If your child has been identified as having difficulty reading or you suspect he or she may have difficulty, it's worth talking to the teacher about the specific intervention options that are available and finding out whether a phonologically based intervention is an option.

[Bennett A. Shaywitz et al., 'Development of left occipitotemporal systems for skilled reading in children after a phonologically based intervention', *Biological Psychiatry*, vol. 55, 2004, pp. 926–33.]

## 72. Fostering healthy approaches to learning

At a time when there's so much emphasis on making sure our kids get a good education, it's important to encourage achievement in healthy ways so as not to create unrealistic expectations, performance anxiety and unhelpful forms of perfectionism.

Parents of academically gifted kids are sometimes stereotyped as being pushy but, for the majority of top students, this is not the case.

If you've got an academically able child, some of the ways you can help them:

- encouraging them to do well
- getting personally involved in educational activities
- providing stimulating opportunities so they can be challenged and develop their talents.

Basically, when it comes to the parents of the gifted, there are two different types: 'performance parents' and 'learning parents'.

Performance parents tend to focus on exam results and academic prizes. Some even see exceptional performance in their intelligent child as a way of achieving social status. These parents are more likely to be critical of mistakes and have unrealistically high standards. While setting moderately high standards has been shown to facilitate performance, unrealistically high expectations can have the reverse effect. A combination of high parental expectations and a strong desire to please can result in a child believing that love and acceptance are entirely dependent on their academic success. Perfectionism has been associated with depression, anorexia, bulimia, obsessive compulsive disorder, migraines and even suicidal tendencies.

That said, perfectionism is not always unhealthy. In talented students, high standards and the perseverance to pursue them can simply be the hallmarks of a gifted, healthy achiever rather than a neurotic, maladjusted perfectionist with pushy parents.

'Learning parents' want their kids to enjoy learning, improve their skills and challenge themselves. While these parents recognise the importance of achievement, they are less inclined to demand high performance at the risk of their child misunderstanding material or suffering performance anxiety. But this strategy has its flaws too. Learning parents are more likely to have children with low personal standards, low levels of organisation, low perceived parental expectations and a tendency to be distractible, potentially hampering future achievement.

Basically it is best not to have expectations that are excessively high or too low. Parents who are critical of mistakes and have unrealistically high expectations and who focus on marks, degrees, prestigious jobs and high salaries are more likely to end up with children who doubt themselves, procrastinate, avoid new learning strategies and underachieve, and who are moody, defensive and anxious. Try to encourage your kids with high—but not unrealistically high—standards while at the same time fostering independence, intellectual growth, self-motivation, understanding and the love of a good challenge.

[Karen E. Ablard & Wayne D. Parker, 'Parents' achievement goals and perfectionism in their academically talented children', *Journal of Youth and Adolescence*, vol. 26, no. 6, 1997, pp. 651–67.]

## 73. Don't see red before a test

No wonder Little Red Riding Hood couldn't tell her grandmother from a fanged carnivore—the colour of her cape impaired her thinking. Red is fabulous at weddings and cocktail parties, but it's not so good for school on test days. Even a brief glimpse of red before a test can impair performance, without kids even realising it.

Colours have a powerful effect on us that we can feel, but don't really understand—which is why you would never paint your bedroom black. When you see red, the right part of your brain becomes active, which is where you feel negative emotions like stress, fear and anger. This could be biological—lots of animals use red to either attract or warn. Or it could be cultural—from an early age we learn to associate red with stoplights, alarms, warnings and danger signs. Add this to the red pen teachers usually use to highlight incorrect answers and you get a colour that can de-motivate people and may make them feel anxious about failing.

Dress your kids in blue, or a similarly soothing colour. You don't have to strip the crimson wallpaper in the bathroom or confiscate toy fire trucks; it's what kids see right before the test that counts. Make sure the school isn't using red cover pages for exams or red pencils, and that the test isn't anywhere near the school theatre with the red velvet curtains.

*Four experiments demonstrate that the brief perception of red prior to an important test (for example, an IQ test) impairs performance, and this effect appears to take place outside of participants' conscious awareness. When high school and undergraduate students either had a red number written at the top of their test pages, or a red cover sheet on an IQ test, they did 20 to 50 per cent worse than students who were exposed in the same way to green, black, grey and white.*

[A.J. Elliot et al., 'Color and psychological functioning: the effect of red on performance attainment', *Journal of Experimental Psychology: General*, *136* (1), 2007, pp. 154–68.]

## 74. Popularity—the good, the bad and the ugly

Remember the days of the old schoolyard? We used to laugh a lot . . . unless we were the ones who used to cry a lot.

In every playground there are popular kids, not-so-popular kids, ringleaders, followers and 'social rejects'. Most kids want to be popular, and most parents want their kids to be popular so as to avoid rejection and loneliness. But what exactly is popularity and how does it arise?

The two main types of popularity are 'sociometric popularity' and 'perceived popularity'. Sociometric popularity refers to kids whose popularity comes from being genuinely nice and kind. Perceived popularity is often derived from a combination of niceness with intimidating and/or manipulative behaviour. These 'cool kids' tend to be ring-leaders who are socially powerful, widely imitated, emulated and possibly feared, though not necessarily well liked on a personal level. Sociometrically popular kids may not be as well known or notorious but they are generally better liked (rather than feared).

When it comes to your kids, ask yourself: Do they have nice friends? Are they kind to other kids? If so, great—studies show that sociometrically popular kids tend to be emotionally well adjusted and have good friendships that last into later life. The 'cool kids', on the other hand, while benefiting in the short term from their ability to manipulate people and get what they want, may suffer when they move into the real world and are recognised as bullies.

Even if your child does seem a bit more of a 'bully' than

'buddy', don't panic. If you can help them find a balance between their nice side and their nasty side, they may be able to continue their reign as successful, influential leaders throughout their lives.

[Antonius H.N. Cilessen & Amanda J. Rose, 'Understanding popularity in the peer system', *Current Directions in Psychological Science*, vol. 14, no. 2, 2005, pp. 102–5.]

## 75. Best friend—or worst?

We all want our kids to have friends and many of us are willing to accept the less than delightful habits they tend to copy from their companions. The odd swear word, backchat or acts of defiance are all hazards of the playground that they might pick up along with the colds and flus.

But what if your child's BFF is psychotic? Or worse, academically unmotivated? What if they spend more time in the principal's office than in the classroom? Will their behaviour rub off on your child?

It depends. Are they best friends or just friends? If they are just friends, their delinquent behaviour is unlikely to turn your child into a fellow delinquent. But if there is a strong attachment between them, there might be cause for concern.

It's worth keeping an eye out for friendships with high levels of conflict and aggression, since this can lead to disruptive and disagreeable behaviour in your child, not just with their friends but with other kids, adults and authority figures. Of course, many friendships have a little rivalry and struggles for dominance but the less there is, the better.

Hanging out with shy or withdrawn kids will not necessarily make your child more shy or withdrawn. But high-conflict friendships can definitely lead to shy and withdrawn behaviour.

The best kind of friendships your child can have are thoughtful, supportive, warm and giving ones. They will help them develop socially and be incredibly rewarding. But contrary to popular belief, good friends can't help with your child's self-esteem. That's something that has to come from within.

> *Kids involved in friendships with high levels of conflict, rivalry and dominance display increased disruptive and disagreeable behaviours with both their friends and other peers, adults and authority figures. It seems that the interactional style practised amongst the 'friends' becomes habitual, generalising to interactions with others.*
>
> *While having high-quality friendships does enhance a child's perceived social success and acceptance amongst peers, it doesn't necessarily lead to higher self esteem. Hanging out with shy or socially withdrawn kids doesn't necessarily make kids more shy and withdrawn themselves. The effect varies depending on the quality of the friendship; with a tendency for shy and withdrawn behaviour to increase in lower quality friendships, while the support and intimacy shared in higher quality friendship offset tendencies to mimic patterns of withdrawn social behaviour.*

[Thomas Berndt, 'Friendship quality and social development', *Current Directions in Psychological Science*, vol. 11, no. 1, February 2002, pp. 7–10.]

## 76. Bullying doesn't pay

Bullying is a dirty word, but buried deep in some parents is the smug pride that their offspring is obviously rising to be the alpha of the pack, and that dominance in the playground will prepare them for a career as the CEO of a multinational company. You might hear offhand bragging like, 'Oh, no one messes with my Alice. She kicked a boy twice her size in the balls when he tried to cheat in hopscotch.'

Kids bully for all sorts of reasons. Maybe they have problems at home and take their frustrations out on other kids. Maybe they were once bullied themselves and now they have the chance to turn the tables.

But while little Alice may rule uncontested in the playground, being kingpin isn't all it's cracked up to be. Regardless of gender, aggressive children are more likely to be unhappy than other children. They are also twice as likely to feel left out, have a difficult time enjoying themselves and have a poor self-image.

Most schools have a zero-tolerance policy approach to bullying, but the definition of bullying is fairly elastic. Is it only physical abuse? What about verbal abuse? Or breaking another kid's pens, or making faces at someone in the corridor? The truth is, the more subtle nuances of bullying often get overlooked. Parents have to be more insistent on a firm anti-bullying policy in the school and make sure the bullying policy is enforced.

Teach your kids from a young age to play nice. Teach them that picking on people is mean and unacceptable, and that bullying, whether verbal or physical, is no way to make friends and influence people. Their happiness depends on it.

[D. Glover et al., 'Bullying in 25 secondary schools: incidence, impact and intervention', *Educational Research*, 42 (2), 2000, pp. 141–56. J.B. Sprott, & A.N. Doob, 'Bad, sad and rejected: the lives of aggressive children', *Canadian Journal of Criminology*, 42 (2), 2000, pp. 123–33.]

## 77. Race relations in the playground

Research shows that when it comes to children choosing playmates, colour matters quite a lot.

A recent study on the influence of race on playmate choices provides a fresh perspective on how children relate to different racial groups. It also sheds light on how aspects of children's identity influence their conversations, friendships and peer relationships, and what effect mixing with different groups has on prejudice.

In general, interpersonal contact between different races may reduce prejudice and create good race relations. However, if such contact creates negative forms of interactions or further reinforces stereotypes, it may be of questionable value.

The kids in the study were aged seven to eight, an important age in terms of racial understanding since kids tend to hold negative attitudes towards 'out-groups' from early childhood. These start to become more positive from around age seven, though kids this age still don't tend to seek out kids from other racial groups, perhaps as a result of the more powerful effects of peer pressure to make same-race, 'in-group' friendship choices.

The researchers found that race influences a child's conversation style, with kids of European descent tending to be more assertive than those of South Asian or African-Caribbean descent, and kids of South Asian descent tending to be more accommodating and supportive than European kids. It is thought that European kids may learn more assertive conversational styles from their parents and peers, while South Asian kids learn to be more accommodating.

Despite displaying a more assertive style in the study, European kids did not necessarily dominate or assert themselves over minority-group kids. It is possible that this result might vary with the racial mix at a school and the degree to which that school celebrates its racial diversity (or lack thereof).

Same-race pairs of kids (regardless of their race) tended to choose same-race playmates, though this was less marked amongst the minority-group races.

Pairs of friends of differing races had more difficulty agreeing on a choice of playmate, and when they did agree they were inclined to choose a European child, perhaps because racial-minority kids tend to favour a playmate from what they perceive to be a higher status group.

To reduce racial prejudice, it is important to challenge kids' existing friendship preferences and to encourage interaction with children from different groups, as well as fostering positive interactions. Racially neutral tasks such as free play, problem-solving and collaborative learning provide good opportunities for kids from different groups to interact positively and might help to prevent friendship choices influenced by race from becoming ingrained in early childhood.

Race is a powerful force that affects not only kids' choice of playmates but the dynamics and outcome of their conversations. Encouraging friendly cross-racial play and activities, as well as doing our best to reduce the perceived dominance of a particular racial group and being aware of how your own behaviour reinforces this, could help to create a world where it really does not matter if you're black, white or brindle.

[Patrick J. Leman & Virginia L. Lam, 'The influence of race and gender on children's conversations and playmate choices', *Child Development*, vol. 79, no. 5, Sept/Oct 2008, pp. 1329–43.]

## 78. How shy is too shy?

We all get shy. A room full of people we don't know is enough to prick feelings of anxiety in most of us, and it's no different for children. But when does shyness become a problem?

A little clinginess during the first ten minutes of a birthday party is no cause for concern. And sometimes kids prefer to play alone, and that's okay too. But if your child seems to be deliberately excluded by other children, becomes anxious and fearful every time another child appears, and regularly runs away from playtime with others, this kind of shyness can lead to low self-esteem, anxiety, rejection by other kids, and academic difficulties in school.

Not all children who are shy develop problems. But if you are worried, there are a few things you can do to help. From the day your kids are born to the day they get their driver's licence, the main facilitator of their social interactions is you. You are the one who arranges play dates, drives them to sleepovers, and supervises their pool parties. Having friends helps children feel less shy and lonely, and although it can sometimes be a bit of a hassle, you are the one who brings your kids together with these friends. You are also the one who listens to endless stories of who is the current BFF, who just got kicked out of the circle of trust, and what Janet's mum said. Reading to your kids and encouraging them to read also helps, as this improves their vocabulary so they can better express themselves.

Most importantly, don't be too controlling of your children. Let them make mistakes and figure things out for themselves. Also, make sure they feel loved. If they feel rejected by you, they are more likely to fear rejection by everyone else.

*In the preschool years, shyness is related to poorer social competence, lower self-esteem, anxiety, peer rejection, increased teacher attention, and academic difficulties. Increased verbal skills may be particularly important in facilitating social interactions for shy children. In addition, parental rejection and control (that is, over-control, lack of encouragement of independence) appears to exacerbate the negative outcomes of shyness.*

[R.J. Coplan & M. Armer, 'A "multitude" of solitude: a closer look at social withdrawal and non social play in early childhood', *Child Development Perspectives*, *1* (1), 2007, pp. 26–32. L. Greco & T. Morris, 'Treating childhood shyness and related behavior: empirically evaluated approaches to promote positive social interaction', *Clinical Child and Family Psychology Review*, *4* (4), 2001, pp. 299–318.]

## 79. Only the lonely . . .

It's normal for a child to feel lonely from time to time. Maybe their best friend has moved away, or has glandular fever and can't play with anyone for six weeks.

However, if they complain about being lonely a lot then you may have cause for concern, as chronic loneliness can lead to a whole range of problems later in life including dropping out of school, depression, alcoholism and health issues.

Children who are picked on by other kids suffer more loneliness than those who are rejected but not overtly victimised. Withdrawn, rejected kids report more loneliness than aggressive, rejected kids. If your child falls into either category, think about ways you can intervene to break the cycle, such as by teaching them good social skills appropriate to their age (how to be a good friend, how to share, how to listen).

But even kids with lots of friends can suffer from loneliness. This may be because they have unrealistic expectations of their friends, for example, that they will never let them down, hurt their feelings or break a promise. So it's important to teach kids early that sometimes people make mistakes. If your children can learn how to share, to offer and accept companionship, help and intimacy, and to make up after a fight, this will set them on the path to feeling much less lonely.

*Kids with 'high quality' enduring friendships, featuring high degrees of companionship, help, guidance, intimacy and ease of conflict-resolution, generally experience less loneliness. Kids whose friendships feature high degrees of relational aggression (ignoring the 'friend' when angry, attempting to influence the 'friend' by threatening termination of the friendship) experience more loneliness. Chronic loneliness can be associated with various indices of maladjustment (including depression, dropping out, alcoholism). A true loner might not feel lonely despite being alone and even being widely rejected, whereas a different sort of person might feel lonely despite being surrounded by many friends.*

[Steven R. Asher & Julie A. Paquette, 'Loneliness and peer relations in childhood', *Current Directions in Psychological Science*, vol. 12, no. 3, June 2003, pp. 75–8.]

## 80. Imaginary friends

You might try to keep a careful eye on who your kids play with, but what if their BFF is a green dog named Captain Comet, who dies if he doesn't get a treat every five minutes? Aren't imaginary friends just for lonely kids who can't find real ones?

Relax. Your child's emotional development can be enhanced by imaginary friends, whether they are male, female or of unknown, indeterminate gender. They could be human, animal or other; magical, exotic or 'ordinary'; visible or invisible; embodied in a toy, stuffed animal or doll. They can even be the child's own reflection in the mirror. The relationship might be one of a close confidant they share their thoughts and feelings with, a playmate, or even someone who is alternately friendly or mean.

The great thing about imaginary friends is that your child has to imagine the thoughts and feelings of someone whose beliefs and intentions are different from their own. This is an important skill that will help them manage all sorts of social situations. In fact, children who have imaginary friends tend to do better at guessing other people's thoughts and feelings than children who don't.

As for the idea that kids with imaginary friends are lonely or losers—it's actually quite the opposite. Kids who create imaginary companions are generally more sociable, more creative, participate in more family activities and are more likely to get on well with others. High levels of fantasy in the play of children aged four to eight was correlated with higher self-ratings of peer acceptance.

Kids as old as twelve and even adolescents can have imaginary friends. In fact, socially competent, creative adolescents with good coping skills are more likely to refer to imaginary companions in their diaries.

So please welcome any of your children's imaginary friends into your homes, gardens, closets and spaces under the bed. They help develop your children's awareness of and sensitivity to other people's perspectives and will make your kids more sociable, socially capable and creative. Best of all, imaginary friends don't cost anything to feed, don't make any mess and don't occupy an extra car booster seat.

*More children (31%) are playing with imaginary characters at age seven than at preschool age (28%), although adults tended to be less aware of them since they were more likely to be invisible and the nature of the imaginary play tends to be less overt and is sometimes deliberately secretive.*

[Marjorie Taylor et al., 'The characteristics and correlates of fantasy in school-age children: Imaginary companions, impersonation and social understanding', *Developmental Psychology*, vol. 40, no. 6, 2004, pp. 1173–87.]

## 81. Getting through the tough times

You can't protect your kids from all the bad stuff in life. Sometimes, really sad things happen that are beyond your control, like a grandparent dying, a cyclone blowing the house down, or an accident that involves a trip to the hospital.

Chances are that you'll be a wreck yourself. So it's worth knowing that the way you talk about a stressful event influences the way your children remember it. Parents have a huge influence on the way memories are formed in their children's minds; those who remember events with rich detail pass these memories on to their children, so they remember them that way too.

For a stressful event, it's helpful for children to know the how and the why. What was the chain of events that lead up to the stressful occurrence? Who was there to help? How did it turn out? Well? Most importantly, talk about your emotions in a positive light if you can, for example, 'I was very upset and frightened when you broke your leg, but I knew it was going to be okay' or 'I'm so sad Grandma isn't here any more but I know she loved you and was so proud of you, and she made the best chocolate cake in the world'.

The worst thing you can do is pretend it never happened. Children who internalise stress usually end up with behavioural problems later on.

Life isn't perfect, and occasionally it can be downright rotten. But accepting the bad along with the good is important for dealing with future crises, and turns us into stronger and better people.

*Children, who are still in the process of developing autobiograph-*
*ical memory skills, may be especially dependent on others to help*
*them construct and evaluate coherent memories of stressful events.*
*In a study of 8–12 year old children, mothers who talk more*
*about emotions and provide more explanations in discussions of*
*the chronic stressor have children who display fewer behavioural*
*problems such as depression, anxiety and aggression.*

[J.M. Sales & R. Fivush, 'Social and emotional functions of mother-child reminiscing about stressful events', *Social Cognition*, *23* (1), 2005, pp. 70–90.]

## 82. Helping your chickens cross the road

As a parent, you should think of cars as stampeding water buffalo, and roads as crocodile-infested rivers. Getting hit by a car is the leading cause of death amongst Australian children from the age of one to fourteen years old. What can you do to help them make it safely to the other side?

Crossing the road requires a range of skills that don't fully develop until children become teenagers. They have to be able to distinguish a safe road crossing from a dangerous one, which young children have difficulty with. They have to concentrate on the situation without getting distracted by a million other things (their friends yelling, a dog barking). They also have to quickly switch their attention from one thing to another (the colour of the traffic lights, and cars approaching from different directions).

Basically, children should not cross roads unsupervised until they are ten years old. Kids under ten are difficult for motorists to see, are slower than adults so they can't get out of the way fast enough, have difficulty judging the distance and speed of cars, and have underdeveloped peripheral vision. Even after they turn ten, children may know how to be safe but are still prone to reckless behaviour.

To teach road safety, instead of relying on a set of rules like 'look right, look left, look right', interact with your child. Ask them when they think it is a good time to cross, then give them instant feedback. Talk about safe places to cross like zebra crossings and traffic signals, but teach them to pay attention to what the traffic is doing regardless of where they cross.

And hold their hand tightly. If they are going to take on crocodiles, they need to be well protected.

*Young children have most difficulty in identifying 'dangerous' sites and are more likely to say that a dangerous site is safe than they are to say a 'safe' crossing site is dangerous. The ability to identify safe and dangerous road-crossing sites increased with age up to age 10 to 11 years. Although 10 to 11-year-olds appear to have reached adult levels of ability at identifying safe and dangerous crossing sites, they take longer to do so than adults.*

[D.S. Cross & M.R. Hall, 'Child pedestrian safety: the role of behavioural science', *182* (7), 2005, p. 2. Z. Tabibi & K. Pfeffer, 'Finding a safe place to cross the road: the effect of distractors and the role of attention in children's identification of safe and dangerous road-crossing sites', *Infant and Child Development, 16* (2), 2007, pp. 193–206.]

## 83. Walkin' the dog

Childhood obesity is a complex issue, but physical activity clearly has a role to play. And recent studies have found that owning a dog can greatly increase kids' level of physical activity.

Having a dog increases the physical activity of dog owners, with some studies showing that people with dogs walk almost twice as much as those without. And young girls in families with a dog spend around half an hour more each day doing physical activity than those without a pooch at home. Other studies show that children aged five to six in families who own a dog are half as likely to be overweight or obese compared to those who do not.

As well as increasing the amount of activity a child is getting via ball-throwing, wrestling, chasing and being chased, owning a dog has other benefits. A dog is a companion and a valued friend. For kids, 'playing with pets' rated just behind 'playing with friends' as their favourite activity. And having a dog may inadvertently help your child make friends given that stigmatisation by other kids against overweight or obese kids is present by age six, with obese children and adolescents described by their peers as the least desired friends.

A well-trained dog is the perfect judgment-free, always-adoring companion who encourages healthy levels of physical activity. And a possible bodyguard to boot. For some parents, the presence of the family dog can alleviate concerns about safety when walking in the park or neighbouring streets. This probably depends on the size and temperament of the dog, but it can mean getting out of the house more at least, which is a good thing.

Of course, when considering whether or not to get a dog, other aspects such as safety need to be taken into account, in particular when considering the size, breed and nature of the dog. Risk of bites and other serious injuries from being attacked need to be taken seriously, so it's worth talking to a professional and getting advice on what type of dog might be best for your family, lifestyle and expectations.

[Anna Timperio et al., 'Is dog ownership or dog walking associated with weight status in children and their parents?' *Health Promotion Journal of Australia* 2008: vol. 19, no. 1, pp. 60–3.]

## 84. Play hard

Kids need playtime, but certain kinds of play are more effective than others.

Surprisingly, playing outdoors can lead to poor school marks and behaviour problems. While 'go outside and play' is good in small doses, it lacks the competitive, goal-oriented aspect of playing organised sport. Skateboarding and riding bikes tend to be unstructured and unorganised and don't require any discipline, effort or teamwork. Also, outside play and 'hanging out' often involve no adult supervision and might turn into hanging outside toilets bumming cigarettes.

Hobbies and sports are the most likely structured activities to decrease depression and increase academic performance. The discipline, self-direction and sense of competence that comes from working on a hobby or playing a sport creates a sense of industry important to development. Unfortunately, watching TV, playing a DS and other kinds of passive activities don't count as hobbies.

So get your kids interested in something that requires training and has milestones to mark their progress, whether it's the next belt in karate or a rare stamp for their collection. It will make them feel good about themselves and may even improve their results at school.

[S.M. McHale, A.C. Crouter & C.J. Tucker, 'Free-time activities in middle childhood: links with adjustment in early adolescence', *Child Development*, 72 (6), 2001, pp. 1764–78.]

## 85. Make sure they get enough zzzz . . .

Enforcing bedtimes is one of the most important things you can do to help your children at school. Children who don't get enough sleep have worse attention, concentration and test scores than children who sleep well. This is especially true for younger children. Sleep deprivation can lead to behaviour problems that mimic symptoms of ADHD, like extreme impulsivity. And poor sleep is even linked to asthma and atopic dermatitis (eczema).

Just like grown-ups, kids don't sleep well if they're anxious. This can result in a chicken-and-egg situation where kids get less sleep if they're anxious and they become more anxious with less sleep. This in turn affects their performance at school.

Family stress is one of the main causes of anxiety, so do everything in your power to make the home a calm, stress-free environment. Since school generally always starts at the same time, make sure they get to bed early enough so they aren't anxious about not having enough hours sleep till morning. Make sure they exercise to give them a better chance of a solid night's rest.

Read them a story, tuck them in, tell them everything is alright and leave them with pleasant, soothing thoughts. This basic form of meditation can help them feel less anxious before they go to sleep so they will wake up bright and refreshed.

[A.M. Gregory & T.C. Eley, 'Sleep problems, anxiety and cognitive style in school-aged children', *Infant and Child Development*, *14* (5), 2005, pp. 435–44. A. Sadeh, R. Gruber & A. Raviv, 'Sleep, neurobehavioral functioning, and behavior problems in school-age children', *Child Development*, *73* (2), 2002, pp. 405–17.]

## 86. Sleep problems in kids and teens

When they're tiny babies, many of us worry about them getting to sleep and staying asleep. In the toddler years we fret over their refusal to go to bed, and then as their schedule becomes increasingly packed with various activities and commitments, we worry about them not getting enough rest. But who would have guessed that in middle childhood and adolescence we'd be worrying about them sleeping too much? Believe it or not, after all that time wishing they would go to bed and stay there, for some parents things can go from one extreme to the other.

For many kids, sleeping in on weekends or holidays or any other time they are not overbooked with activities is simply a great way to make up for lost between-the-sheets time. However, if their sleeping patterns shift and they start sleeping a lot more than usual, napping in the afternoon or after dinner, having trouble waking up or getting out of bed and still feeling sleepy nearly all day every day, there's a chance they may have hypersomnia.

Unfortunately, while you may be enjoying the peace and quiet, this Rip Van Winkle phenomenon can have serious significance, and while other possible underlying causes need to be ruled out (for example, narcolepsy, sleep apnoea and chronic fatigue syndrome), a diagnosis of hypersomnia, like insomnia, is associated with the more severe forms of depression.

Sleep, sleep quality and sleep quantity are enduringly important aspects of well-being far beyond the cradle, with important neurobiological mechanisms existing between sleep and mood, weight change and activity. Keeping an eye on how much and how well our kids sleep is vital to monitoring their overall health and well-being, both physical and emotional—and it's not simply a case of 'the more the merrier'. Hypersomnia or excessive sleeping and daytime sleepiness is just as much a cause for concern as insomnia, and the two conditions co-existing together in an alternating or chaotic fashion (for example, not sleeping or having difficulty falling or staying asleep one night, followed by sleeping way too much the next, or being sleepy all the time during the day and napping during daylight hours) is an even bigger worry.

Don't ignore any kind of sleep disturbance or sleep difficulty, especially if it is combined with excessive daytime sleepiness and prolonged or excessive sleep, and even more crucially if it occurs in association with depressive symptoms. Seek medical advice and don't let your concerns be too quickly dismissed as 'just what teenagers do'.

*Sleep disturbances are very common in depressed children, with 73 per cent of depressed children in this study having either insomnia or hypersomnia. This study of 553 children aged 7 to 15 with major depression found that 53 per cent had insomnia alone, 9 per cent had hypersomnia alone and 10 per cent had both hypersomnia and insomnia. The highest depression severity was observed in children with both types of sleep disturbance and the lowest severity was in children with neither sleep disturbance. In addition, sleep disturbance correlated with specific depressive symptoms: hypersomnia correlated with weight loss, weight gain and a sense of worthlessness; and insomnia with depressed mood, diurnal variation (variation in symptoms across the course of the day) and agitation. Combined hypersomnia and insomnia was associated with anhedonia (loss of joy or pleasure in things), weight loss, agitation, distinct sadness and guilt. In addition, children with sleep disorders were more likely to have co-existing anxiety disorders.*

[Xianchen Liu et al., 'Insomnia and hypersomnia associated with depressive phenomenology and co-morbidity in childhood depression', *Sleep* 2007; vol. 30, no. 1, pp. 83–90.]

## 87. What do they do all day?

For many adults, there is never enough leisure time. For adolescents, however, other than attending school, very little else is totally compulsory. They can do paid work, homework, hang out with friends either in person or online, or take part in extracurricular activities. By and large the choice is theirs, and the choices they make may not only help define their identities and life roles in the present, but also what they do in the future.

Adolescence is a time when kids are expanding their social world; exploring possible identities, social roles, relationships and wider possibilities. By engaging in a variety of roles, adolescents broaden their social contacts and support networks and are exposed to new opportunities and challenges.

Finding a job as a teenager provides exposure to the adult world of work and may promote a positive self-image. Some students involved in paid work are able to find a balance whereby considerable time is devoted to a range of activities: school and school-related activities, work, friends and family.

But not all kids are able to achieve this balance. Several studies have linked paid work with kids dropping out of school early. Then there are those kids who are not highly engaged with either school or paid work, and who spend increasing amounts of time alone or with peers in unstructured settings.

How our kids choose to spend their time is not a random affair. Their choices reflect their aspirations for the future as well as what they are most comfortable doing. Kids who don't enjoy school and feel they have failed to thrive in that environment will seek and focus on other areas, which means an increased chance that they will drop out of school too early, missing out on a lot of the extracurricular benefits school can offer.

Gender and social class also have an impact on how adolescents spend their time. Even in adolescence, girls spend more time doing household tasks. And while boys spend more of their leisure time on sports, girls tend to engage in less structured leisure such as chatting to friends on the phone. Family socioeconomic status may have a strong influence on kids' educational plans and career aspirations too, with kids from wealthier socioeconomic backgrounds tending to adopt time-use patterns that are associated with greater school success.

Those kids who are able to maintain a wide variety of interests and activities—both in and out of school— benefit from exposure to a range of experiences and social interactions with both peers and adults. They also tend to have more optimistic outlooks and positive future plans regarding career, citizenship and relationships.

So while it's good for kids to be involved in doing household chores and paid work, ideally this should not be at the expense of other age-appropriate activities such as sport, debating, dance, music, chess, homework, hobbies and spending time with friends.

It's worth encouraging kids to find balance in the way that they spend their time. In general, being highly engaged tends to augur well compared to being largely disengaged, and high involvement in school-related activities such as homework and extracurricular commitments (such as the school musical, choir, chess and orchestra) is a good sign too. Kids who seem to be veering away from such school-related activities and throwing themselves into paid work, chores or other unstructured activities (such as hanging out with friends) may be at high risk of dropping out of school too early.

You can't necessarily control what your kids get up to but you can at least keep an eye out for worrying trends. School-age kids in general do best when they stay in school and engage, at least to some degree, in school-related activities, both for the activities themselves and the social experiences. If your child is fleeing the school arena because of past negative experiences, it is worth trying to find at least some area of school life where he or she can shine, or at least feel some sense of comfort, self-esteem and belonging.

As adults, it is good if we can ourselves model a healthy lifestyle balance to our children and, failing that, at least recognise when our kids are too narrowly focused on certain pastimes to the exclusion of other potentially beneficial ones.

[Michael J. Shanahan & Brian P. Flaherty, 'Dynamic patterns of time use in adolescence', *Child Development*, vol. 72, no. 2, March/April 2001, pp. 385–40.]

## 88. Gaming into the future

Computer games. Most kids love them; you might hate them. But are they really the soulless suckers of time, hypnotising your kids and inculcating them in violent, sexist practices and power-based hierarchies, that some of us fear?

Unfortunately, some of the harshest critics of computer games often have very little personal experience of the excitement and intellectual stimulation that gaming can bring, or of the variety of themes, cultures and social 'worlds' gaming encompasses.

Boys tend to be involved more often and at more sophisticated levels with gaming than girls. From as early as preschool, boys can spend hours playing these games, puzzling their way through engrossing and interactive texts. Far from being a waste of time, your child may well be enjoying a different form of learning, increasing his understanding of popular new media while developing the skills and confidence to negotiate digital spaces and new technological tools.

A recent study looked at a group of year 11 and 12 high-school students learning to create their own computer games as an entry point to learning the abstract concepts of computer programming. The students had a varied level of ability and experience: some had rarely played computer games while others were considering careers in the industry.

During the exercise, a real sense of community developed. The kids were deeply immersed in problem-solving, independently seeking out, trialling and then testing solutions before looking for new ones if necessary. Rather than raising their hands to ask for help, the kids wrote their names on a whiteboard and then continued seeking solutions for themselves. Teachers reported that in half the cases students had already solved their problems before the teacher got to them, a gratifying outcome for both teachers and students.

The process of making computer games encouraged and actually required kids to be willing to reach out and seek new tools beyond traditional textbooks or teacher-given notes to help themselves learn better, supporting development of the skills required for lifelong learning well beyond the classroom.

The kids seemed completely absorbed in their new task, often settling down to work before the bell went and spending their spare time getting feedback (as well as giving feedback to other kids) on what their games were like to play. Along with the actual making of the games, the kids enjoyed and benefited from the social support, encouragement and constructive criticism they received from their peers, with many making changes, improvements and modifications to their games as a result of this feedback.

Making and playing computer games inherently involves a great deal of social networking. Gamers share a language, a passion and a socially accepted culture and way of behaving and interacting. Kids found the exercise of creating their own computer game challenging and hugely satisfying, many comparing learning programming language to learning a foreign language—one that allowed them to create a product anyone could play.

Computer games bring with them new forms of literacy and are only just starting to be recognised as forms of media worthy of studying at school. Reading is to writing as computer-game playing is to computer-game creation. Many more people will read and appreciate books than will ever write or publish one, and the same goes for gaming. Being able to savour the craftsmanship and having some understanding of what might be involved in the creation adds to the enjoyment.

So if playing computer games is your child's first love, it's not necessarily a waste of time. Computer games are a burgeoning popular media for which there is growing demand—not just for greater quantity but for quality. Not every computer-game fanatic will create the next gaming sensation, but along the way they may well develop new technical and social skills that help equip them for what lies ahead.

[Kathy Sanford & Leanna Madill, 'Recognizing new literacies: Teachers and students negotiating the creation of video games in school', DiGRA (Digital Games Research Association) 2007 conference paper, pp. 583–9.]

## 89. The upside of computer games

The widespread prevalence and popularity of computer games, especially amongst boys, has prompted concerns about increased aggressive behaviour and thoughts, desensitisation to violence and decreased empathy. Some fear that immersion and interactivity with computer games, compared to more passive media like TV, could blur the players' perceptions of the boundaries between fantasy and reality. They worry that repeated acting out of aggressive scripts within violent games could lead to automatic aggressive responses in real-life situations.

Numerous studies have been conducted in this area, yielding varied and mixed results. But the fact is that despite more and more adolescent boys playing violent computer games over the past decade, the rates of juvenile violent crime—including murder—have been steadily declining, with arrest rates in the US now at their lowest since at least 1980.

There are, of course, other established risk factors for aggressive or violent behaviour, including neurological damage, insecure attachment, parental neglect or abuse, poverty and neighbourhood violence. Reports connecting youth violence to computer games often neglect to take these into account. For example, the lawyer who represented Lee Malvo, an adolescent charged with a series of fatal sniper shootings in the US, cited exposure to computer game violence in the defence of his client. However, Malvo also had a history of parental abandonment, poverty, animal torture and violent attacks with weapons.

In addition to any potential harmful effects, computer games have numerous potential benefits, with studies finding links between interactive game play and social and emotional well-being in adolescents. Computer games provide adolescents with opportunities to explore rules and consequences in novel situations outside their real-life world.

Some researchers suggest that playing computer games may provide a safe outlet for aggressive and angry feelings for some kids, having a beneficial, cathartic effect. In addition, just as boys use rough-and-tumble play to explore aggression and establish 'pack order' by focusing on dominance rather than causing physical harm, they may use computer games in the same way. And just as some boys, but generally only a minority, may engage in physical rough play in a dysfunctional manner, so too may some boys engage with computer games in a dysfunctional way.

Recently researchers interviewed adolescent boys about why they played computer games and what they thought the influence of such games was on their emotions, behaviour, friendships and social lives, as well as their impression of the impact of such games on their peers and younger siblings.

When asked whether they felt the violent content of the games could affect their behaviour or make them more violent, most boys thought that while it might affect others, depending on their maturity, it didn't affect them. Boys could clearly distinguish between what was acceptable in games versus real life, and made clear distinctions between antisocial and violent behaviours that were unlikely to occur in real life (such as using powerful weapons) and those that might (such as swearing, giving attitude, and being rude or intimidating).

In terms of positive influences, the boys reported that computer games, especially role-play games, motivated them to think creatively to solve problems.

For many boys, computer games play an important role in their socialisation, helping them start and maintain friendships and assisting in building self-esteem and gaining acceptance. Indeed, studies of adults and older adolescents have shown that the primary motivator for playing computer games, especially for men, is social interaction.

Boys also reported that gaming provided a safe outlet for less positive feelings. For example: 'Last week . . . my teacher yelled at me. When I went home I started playing *Vice City* . . . I smashed a lot of cars and blew them up. I was mad and I turned happy afterwards.' This use of computer games to regulate emotion, channel anger and relieve stress, as well as to substitute fantasy fights for real-life ones, is supported by a number of other studies. Adolescents use various media, from computer games to music such as heavy metal, to purge anger, calm down and cope with negative moods.

While violent computer games are certainly more popular amongst boys than girls, around 20 per cent of female gamers report frequent use of at least one title in the mature-rated *Grand Theft Auto* series, which ran second only to *The Sims* in popularity amongst girls. Around 29 per cent of girls also reported using games to cope with anger and other emotions. As to why girls seem less interested in violent computer games, female players say it is not so much the violence and death-dealing that puts them off as the male-oriented culture of game players.

While a lot of the discussion around computer games has tended to centre around risks, harm and limiting use, some studies highlight their developmentally appropriate uses: as a safe outlet to express fantasies of power and glory, to explore and master exciting environments, and to work out feelings of stress, anger and frustration, as well as providing a social tool to compete or work cooperatively with peers.

[Cheryl K. Olson et al., 'Role of violent video game content in adolescent development: Boys' perspectives', *Journal of Adolescent Research*, vol. 23, no. 1, 2008, pp. 55–75.]

## 90. Computer-related injuries

We've all suffered from a little RSI (repetitive strain injury) after spending too much time at a computer—the aches and pains that pop up in your hand, arm or neck. Some of us have had RSI that was so serious it became impossible to even pick up a coffee cup.

In this digital age, it is important to be aware that kids can get RSI too. Computers may now be in classrooms, but kids spend the most time on computers when they are at home. Add to this that over 90 per cent of school-aged children have some kind of electronic game at home and you have kids spending between one and two hours a day on a computer and up to an hour a day on video games.

Over half of all children in one study reported being in some kind of pain from using a computer or playing video games. Most reported neck pain, but there were others who said they felt pain in their back and fingers.

Make sure they are using a computer chair and that it is at the appropriate height to the desk (which it won't be if they are using your desk or a common workstation in the house). It's never too early to teach them the right posture and check they have back, arm, feet and wrist support. Encourage them to take frequent breaks (five minutes every fifteen minutes) and teach them hand and wrist exercises to loosen and strengthen muscles. Make sure they aren't spending hours hammering a button (which is the main activity for most video games).

It's hard enough managing RSI in adults. We need to protect our kids and make sure they don't graduate high school with a chronic condition.

[R. Erlynn Mae Ang, A.J. Christine & B.L. Jane, 'Children's computer usage: are they at risk of developing repetitive strain injury?', *Work: A Journal of Prevention, Assessment and Rehabilitation*, 25 (2), 2005, pp. 143–54.]

## 91. Wii versus work

We grew up playing Pacman and Donkey Kong. Now, video games are more like being zapped into an alternative universe, where kids can practise target skills and hone their hand-eye coordination. And there are even *educational* video games.

But kids who spend an hour a day playing video games have less time for real education, like homework and reading. In fact one study showed that for every hour boys spend playing video games, they spend two minutes less reading. This may not sound like much, but when the average amount of time spent reading for boys is only eight minutes per day, this represents a 25 per cent decrease. For every hour girls spend playing video games, they spend thirteen minutes less doing homework (a 30 per cent decrease).

Will playing video games turn your kids into socially isolated computer geeks? Not necessarily, especially if they play with friends. Playing video games with friends is certainly better than playing alone, since video gamers who play with friends are more likely to include friends in other activities. Also, if they play video games with you they are more likely to include you in other activities. This is especially true for girls.

So don't feel any guilt jumping on the Xbox with your kids. Just make sure it's not for too long.

[H.M. Cummings & E.A. Vanderwater, 'Relation of adolescent video game play to time spent in other activities', *Arch Pediatr Adolesc Med*, 161 (7), 2007, pp. 684–9.]

## 92. Attention to detail

We know we just said not to let kids spend too much time playing video games, but we don't want to leave out an important detail: kids who play video games naturally pay more attention to detail.

Usually, the harder you concentrate on one thing, the less attention you have left to notice other things. So if you were concentrating really hard on hitting a ball, you might not notice someone walking her dog nearby.

But it seems people who play video games are able to notice a lot more than non-gamers. While they are hitting a ball they will notice the woman and her dog, as well as a red car passing, as well as a sprinkler going off. People who play video games also notice new objects more quickly. So if, for example, they were watching a boat on the horizon and another boat appeared, they would notice the second boat almost immediately while the brains of non-gamers would take longer to register it.

[C.S. Green & D. Bavelier, 'Action video game modifies visual selective attention', *Nature*, *423* (6939), 2003, pp. 534–7.]

## 93. Violence is as violence does— say no

Though you may want to deliver a hearty smack to a child when you see your priceless Ming vase in shards on the floor, try to resist.

Your parents or others may lecture that there is nothing like a good whopping to drum a lesson into a young brain, and as children grow into the surly, petulant phase of adolescence it may sometimes seem like force is the only way to keep them under control. But children who are severely physically punished are more likely to behave violently towards others. They are also more likely to feel depressed, hopeless, that life has no purpose, and experience other psychological trauma.

Likewise, children who watch their mothers or other people in their family being hit or beaten during an argument learn that it is okay to hit and beat people. Though we mainly see manifestations of this in teenagers, it occurs in children as young as eleven or twelve.

Violent behaviour isn't instinctive—it's learned. Using violence to achieve goals, acquire possessions and resolve conflict is something children pick up from watching those around them. So try to make sure your kids don't watch or experience violence either inside or outside the home. That means living in a safe, non-violent neighbourhood, keeping an eye on your kids to make sure they aren't getting beaten up at school, and screening their music and movies so they aren't absorbing violence from pop culture. Video games where they can blow people's heads off in slow motion may not be so hot either.

And watch out for drugs and cigarettes. Even though many of us got busted for nicking a cigarette from a parent's purse or smoking a joint in the school toilet, it's no time for nostalgia. Substance abuse is more likely to cause violent behaviour in adolescents than being beaten or watching violence.

There's a limit to the control you have over your kids' environment as they grow up, but your home at least should be a sanctuary, somewhere children feel safe. Make it a violence-free zone.

[R.H. DuRant et al., 'Exposure to violence and victimization, depression, substance use, and the use of violence by young adolescents', *The Journal of Pediatrics*, *137* (5), 2000, pp. 707–13.]

## 94. TV rots your brain

Television has become so much a part of our culture that it feels impossible to shelter our children from it. And they go so nice and quiet whenever you put them in front of the telly—it can't be that bad, can it?

Unfortunately it can: there is a growing amount of evidence that ideally children should not watch any television before they are two. We don't know exactly why television is bad for babies and toddlers, but it might be because the more time they spend watching TV, the less time they have for activities like imaginative play, interacting with adults and other children, and exploring their environment. Or it might be that the programs they watch retard their cognitive development. Or maybe it could even be something about the editing, rapid scene changes and looking in one direction at one stimulus for a long time that just isn't good for your baby's brain.

What we do know is that reducing the amount of television six-year-olds watch improves their attention span and IQ. First-graders who watch a lot of television are less able than other students to develop their story-writing skills. And television and DVDs discourage reflection and repress imagination and creativity.

Children who watch excessive amounts of television can become aggressive, obese, and have problems paying attention and sleeping. Watching hours of television in children younger than three can have a negative impact on reading skills, an effect that can last until they are six or seven years old. The problem is that currently there is no appropriate television for children three years old and younger, yet two-thirds of children under the age of two watch over an hour of television a day.

For children three to five years old, there is bad TV and better TV (*Sesame Street* is better than *Prison Break*). But while children in this age group might benefit in letter recognition and short-term memory from *Sesame Street*, there are no benefits to mathematics or reading comprehension.

[F.J. Zimmerman & D.A. Christakis, 'Children's television viewing and cognitive outcomes: a longitudinal analysis of national data', *Archives of Pediatrics and Adolescent Medicine*, *159* (7), 2005, pp. 619–25.]

## 95. Violence on the box

Basically, there are good television programs and bad ones. Good television includes documentaries and educational programs that can widen general knowledge and reinforce what your children learn at school. Bad television is violent, and there is a lot more violence (and more realistic violence) on television today than there was 50 years ago. On an average school night, kids can see people getting shot at, blown up and cut up—and all before 9 pm.

Kids like watching violence on television because it increases their heart rate and makes them feel excited. But it doesn't do them any favours in the long run. Young people who watch a lot of violence on television are more likely to develop aggressive behaviour, including physical aggression (hurting people and animals) and verbal aggression (screaming and temper tantrums). Not only that, watching violence on television when children are young can lead to violent behaviour years into the future.

*Children who watch violence at the age of five are twice as likely to develop teen aggression. Children who regularly watch informative programs in preschool tend to have higher English, maths and science scores in high school.*

[D.R. Anderson et al., 'VI: Aggression', *Monographs of the Society for Research in Child Development*, vol. 66, 2001, pp. 79–89.]

## 96. Dealing with antisocial teenagers

While many adolescents display various antisocial behaviours, most of these have been abandoned by adulthood with only a small percentage continuing with risky, aggressive and violent behaviour. In this small minority, moral disengagement plays a key role in them sanctioning their own actions.

Our principles and morals are shaped by both our own experiences and the experiences of others. During adolescence, the ability to regulate impulsive behaviour increases, with less reliance on the external regulation of parents, teachers and other adults. As adolescents work out their own principles and develop their own moral identity, it is these standards and values that dictate the goals they pursue and how they pursue them, as well as the sorts of actions they will shy away from.

This type of self-sanctioning is vital when learning socially appropriate behaviour, especially in situations where the temptation is to act in our own best interests regardless of possible adverse consequences for others.

However, for some people the development of self-sanctioning doesn't occur. Instead there are various self-exonerating techniques: reconstructing behaviour ('I just happened to be holding the knife when he accidentally slipped and fell onto it'), obscuring involvement in the outcome ('I might have jabbed him in the eye but I think his eye mainly got sore because he rubbed it so much afterwards'), misrepresenting the consequences of actions ('He was bunging it on, he wasn't really that badly hurt') or blaming victims ('She was asking for it'). In this way consequences such as guilt and even personal responsibility can be avoided, allowing all kinds of bad conduct while the individual still supposedly maintains their internalised moral standards. Studies show adolescent boys are more likely to become moral disengagers than adolescent girls.

Generally, levels of moral disengagement decline over the course of time as social, emotional and cognitive skills develop. In one study, this was particularly the case between ages fourteen and sixteen, but less so thereafter to age twenty. Exceptions to this were the 'chronic disengagers', whose levels of moral disengagement did not decline significantly, and the 'late desisters', whose levels of disengagement increased between ages fourteen and sixteen then dropped markedly from age sixteen to twenty.

Individuals who were evaluated by peers as exhibiting higher levels of physical and verbal aggression were far more likely to be in the 'chronic' and 'late desister' groups, and there was a higher proportion of boys in the 'chronic disengagers' group.

Aggression and violence appear to have a key role in chronic disengagement. Kids, usually boys, who display higher levels of aggression and violence in early adolescence are more likely to exhibit these same tendencies in later adolescence, particularly if they show little guilt or self-recrimination. These kids are also more likely to have and sustain higher levels of moral disengagement so that, through a process of self-deception, distortion and misrepresentation, they are able to justify and make excuses for their self-serving behaviour.

The mechanisms of moral disengagement can allow some kids to grow into self-serving adults, claiming all sorts of high-blown moral principles while violating these same principles wholesale without a hint of remorse or shame. Do they say their victims deserved it, are annoying or just don't know how to take a joke? Do they see their teachers, parents, 'peer pressure' or society at large as responsible for their behaviour?

Identifying such tendencies and picking children up on them early is important because it increases their understanding that while they may fool some of the people some of the time, they cannot fool all of the people all of the time. And most importantly, they are ultimately fooling no one but themselves.

[Marinella Paciello et al., 'Stability and change of moral disengagement and its impact on aggression and violence in late adolescence', *Child Development*, vol. 79, no. 5, Sept/Oct 2008, pp. 1288–309.]

## 97. Are your kids using drugs?

For most parents, finding out that their kid is hitting the bottle, the bong, or both, is a cause for alarm. Substance use amongst adolescents is related to a number of social, economic and societal problems, from juvenile delinquency to mental health problems, accidental injury and death. Educational difficulties such as impaired cognitive processing (*can't* think), low motivation and school drop-out rates (don't *want* to think), and academic failure (*didn't* think) can also be associated with substance abuse.

There have been loads of studies looking at which kids are at risk and what can be done about it, and a number of factors have been identified as increasing risk. Being male is one and age is another, with kids in the last two years of high school being the biggest users.

Certain personality factors such as 'behavioural under-control' (rebelliousness, risk-taking, impulsiveness and unconventionality) and 'negative emotionality' (using alcohol or drugs to self-medicate for psychological distress) are also associated with substance abuse, as is having a low commitment to school and other conventional institutions, having a low perception of academic ability and not liking school. Then there are the kids who are using substances because they actually think it'll help them cope, will enhance their performance, reduce tension, and so on.

As parents, you can try to encourage a positive attitude to school and schooling, and you can certainly warn your kids of the negative effects of substance use, but in the end most kids form their own judgments based on their own experiences.

In general, the effect of all the risk factors was significantly moderated by one vital overriding factor: *perceived ease of access and opportunity to use*. In other words, kids will tend to stray if they see an easy opportunity to do so without being caught. So, don't give your kids the money to buy the stuff, and keep an eye on what they are up to and their attitudes, (as well as the attitudes of their friends and peers) when it comes to substance use. Be a role model for prudent behaviour around drugs and alcohol and give realistic insights into the short- and long-term effects. Encourage pride in their school and their engagement with it. And finally, set some limits. Let them know that you are on their case. Your involvement and vigilance can help prevent them sliding down the path of drug-addled ignominy and ruin.

[Kristin E. Voelkl & Michael R. Frone, 'Predictors of substance use at school among high school students', *Journal of Educational Psychology*, vol. 92, no. 3, 2000, pp. 583–92.]

## 98. Body image and self-harm in adolescents

Suicide is a leading cause of death amongst adolescents. And while risk factors such as depression, hopelessness and past suicidal behaviour have, not surprisingly, been identified as valuable indicators, they fail to fully account for the suicide risk in our kids. Attitudes to their bodies, while highly relevant, have not generally been considered as a factor.

Adolescence is characterised by significant physical, emotional and social changes, and poor body image, depression and eating disorders are amongst the most common disorders in this age group. With self-esteem so largely influenced by body image, and self-esteem so closely linked to suicide, it's a factor that deserves more attention. And it's not just girls we need to worry about; up to 40 per cent of males suffer negative body image problems.

Body dissatisfaction also increases the likelihood of self-harming behaviour, with some teenagers developing a general disregard for, or even a sense of distance from, their own bodies. This lack of attachment to their physical self makes the act of self-harming easier and in turn can be related to suicidal behaviour.

As Amy Bransch and Jennifer Muehlenkamp write: 'A dysfunctional view of the body increased self-destructive behaviours and in fact negative body attitudes and feelings predicted suicidal ideation above and beyond the effects of depression, hopelessness and past suicidal behaviour in both males and females. Body care and inclination to look after or pamper the body (versus abuse it or put it at risk of danger) was also a significant predictor of suicide risk.'

It is vital to be aware of dips and dives in our children's self-esteem and it is worth taking some time to focus specifically on their changing body image and attitudes and feelings. Do they regard their body as their temple or trash site? Is it something they worship or revile? Teaching our kids to value, cherish, nourish and nurture themselves inside and out is a crucial part of parenting. Monitoring to what degree they do so may be vital for ensuring not just their quality of life but their respect for living itself.

Talk to your kids, listen to what they say regarding their body image and how they feel about how they look. Encourage and foster positive body image and self-esteem by focussing on their beauty and stengths, not their flaws. Teach them how to care for themselves and encourage them to look after the one precious body they have.

[Amy M. Brausch & Jennifer J. Muehlenkamp, 'Body image and suicidal ideation in adolescents', *Body Image* 4, 2007, pp. 207–12.]

## 99. Keeping kids at school

Life can be tough if you drop out of school early (between the ages of fourteen and sixteen), which is why most parents want their kids to hang in there until the end of year 12. And with good reason, as research has shown that, in general, the earlier adolescents start to take on adult roles and behaviours, the more damage they are likely to do to their success and happiness in later life.

So what can you do to increase the chances of your child staying at school as long as possible?

First, try to encourage your child to invest in and feel a sense of attachment to their school and their teachers. This means discouraging them from running the place down, speaking disparagingly or downright insultingly about the teachers, or mocking the school motto (and obviously not doing any of these yourself!). Choose the best school you can access to suit your child and then take pride in it and encourage your kids to do the same. Children who develop a commitment to succeed in school and who feel a sense of attachment to school are more successful academically.

Second, their results on leaving school are really an accumulation of all those earlier years, going right back to kindy. While it's never too late to start encouraging your kids to try hard academically, you'll obviously get the best results if you can get on board and engage early. You don't need to match your expectations for your kids to your own level of achievement, but research does show that parental expectations of their kids' academic performance is a big factor in predicting their actual achievement. So think big, but remember the emphasis should be on setting personal goals and learning for learning's sake, not on beating their peers and getting the most trophies on the mantel.

Third, try to steer them away from the 'wrong crowd'. Delinquency, not surprisingly, is linked with low academic achievement and early school drop out. And hanging out with a delinquent can see a kid end up in the same place, especially if the low-achiever is their best mate. So it's worth keeping in touch with what your child and their friends are up to. You shouldn't try to actively terminate your child's friendships with less savoury kids (indeed, saying something is *verboten* can often have the reverse effect) so much as encourage the development of other friendship networks with kids who may be a more positive influence.

Fourth, try to discourage them from having sex too early. If they are sexually active, nonetheless, ensure that effective contraception is being used. While teen pregnancy doesn't necessarily prevent a child finishing high school, it has been found to be a consistent predictor of early drop out. And if you're feeling relieved that you only have sons, early sexual activity is related to low academic achievement in *both* sexes.

Fifth, low socioeconomic background is associated with early school drop out. While you may not be able to change your financial circumstances, you *can* encourage your kids to stay in school from an early age, and hopefully protect them against continuing the cycle of poverty.

School's important. Kids spend a large proportion of their waking hours and most of the first two decades of their lives there so it's worth doing all you can to make it a positive and inspiring experience, even if it wasn't especially inspiring for you.

[Robert D. Abbott et al., 'Predictors of early high school dropout: A test of five theories', *Journal of Educational Psychology*, vol. 92, no. 3, 2000, pp. 568–82.]

## 100. Let's talk about sex, baby

Sex should be both a natural and exceptionally rewarding part of life, however timing is crucial. Kids who start having sex at a young age (say, twelve to fourteen years) are far more likely to suffer negative consequences—such as sexually transmitted diseases, unwanted teen pregnancies and involuntary sexual experiences—than peers who wait till they're older to have sex.

Studies have repeatedly found links between being from a 'tough' or 'bad' neighbourhood and risky adolescent sexual outcomes, including inconsistent use of contraceptives and teen childbirth. However, studies investigating the link between such neighbourhood disadvantage and when sexual activity begins have found more complex and varying results.

Gender is certainly a factor. Whereas sexual experimentation is often tacitly encouraged in boys, it isn't in girls. Adolescent girls who become sexually active early not only receive more negative labelling by their peers but are more likely to feel regret and remorse afterwards. Girls, more than boys, are susceptible to influences within their neighbourhood. If they're spending time with peers who have more permissive attitudes towards sex and teen pregnancy, this increases the odds that they will think and act in a similar way.

Teenagers living in 'tough' neighbourhoods are more likely to come from low socioeconomic, separated or divorced families, to move house a lot and to hang out with 'delinquent' peers, often from a different age bracket to themselves. And kids from these poorer neighbourhoods have been found to begin sexual activity at a far younger age, between twelve and thirteen years, compared to their more affluent peers. However, while the rate of sexual activity at age twelve is about 2.5 times higher for adolescent girls from low versus higher socioeconomic status families, these odds decreases as girls gets older, becoming negligible by age fifteen.

The same risk factors were noted for adolescent boys but the magnitude of the effects was generally less marked.

While we may have little or no control over our socio-economic status or the type of neighbourhood we live in, it is generally in our children's interests to maintain stability in a good location wherever possible, to encourage stable friendships with non-delinquent, same-age peers and to ensure adequate parental or other adult supervision, especially if there's any history of bad behaviour.

It is also important not to engender a sense of shame around sex in adolescence, but rather to recognise that while curiosity about sex and sexual feelings is natural, normal and healthy, learning about sex and actually engaging in it are two entirely different things. Early sexual initiation (at age twelve to fourteen, or earlier) is fraught with hazards and should be strongly discouraged.

[Veronique Dupere et al., 'Neighbourhood poverty and early transition to sexual activity in young adolescents: a developmental ecological approach', *Child Development*, vol. 79, no. 5, Sept/Oct 2008, pp. 1463–76.]

## Thank you

Deepest thanks to Sophie Hamley, my literary agent, for introducing Vanessa and me in the first place and most heartfelt thanks to Vanessa for being such a patient, understanding and inspiring co-writer.

Thank you to Louise Thurtell, Jo Paul and Rebecca Kaiser at Allen & Unwin for being so patient and supportive.

Thank you to Erin Keneally, my manager at Mark Morrissey and Associates, for your support, understanding and care for so many years.

Thank you to all my fellow mums (and dads!) who help, support, inspire and encourage me every day, and infinite thanks especially to my most cherished and dear: John Sinn, Cathy Scott, Karen Windybank, Fiona Schmidberger, Geoff Gay, Aine Watkins, Ingrid van Loon, Phill McMartin, Avegail Newman, Lynda Fox, Jennifer Lorance, Anthony Fillbrook, Kate Short, Irene Liu, John Hayson, Sureka Goringe, Stephanie Lane, Angela Carey, Megan Hutchins, Melissa Lahoud, Ashley Hannah, Alex Ryan, Rebecca Stubley, Rebecca Greengarten-Saidman, Kerryn Abagi, Sharyn Ch'ang, Warren and Andrea Ling, Aunty Ching-May, Grace Callahan, Bruce Callahan, Les Sinn, Julia Peres, Trudi Bruins, Julie Rodrigues, May-Lian Lee, Stuart and Vanessa Kirkham, Manjula Rajaratnam, Catherine Andrew, Marisa Johnston, Jo Palaitis, Su Para, Janine Kelly, Diana Goodsall, Mary Chrisant-Kyriakos and Andrea Doney. 'Where would I be . . . where would I go . . . who would I be without your love?'

I would also like to thank Andrew Cree, Deborah Cheung, Lionel Chang and Anand Deva for their wisdom and teaching but most of all their enormous kindness and friendship.

And finally, to my most adored and adorable sons: Anton Huan-De (aka Anakin) and Jeremy Huan-Yu (aka Obi-Wan or Qui-Gon, depending on the day), 'you're the meaning in my life, you're the inspiration, you bring feeling to my life'. Thank you for being so loving, giving, forgiving, funny, gorgeous, inspiring, irrepressible, helpful, caring, tender and sweet and for making my heart melt, grow and glow with pride and joy every day.

*Cindy*